76

TJopling .

CAMBRIDGE REVISITED

B. Leach, delt.

R. H. Leach sculpt.

OLD GARRET HOSTEL BRIDGE
Circa 1810

CAMBRIDGE REVISITED

BY

ARTHUR B. GRAY

E. P. PHELPS. DEL.

ST BENE'T'S TOWER

PATRICK STEPHENS LIMITED
CAMBRIDGE

First published by W. Heffer & Son Ltd in 1921

New edition October 1974

ISBN 0 85059 184 8

Printed by offset lithography on 100 gsm Cartridge paper
at the University Printing House, Cambridge, for the publishers,
Patrick Stephens Ltd, Bar Hill, Cambridge, CB3 8EL,
and bound at the University Printing House, Cambridge.

To the memory
of
ARTHUR JOHN GRAY
Capt 1/1 Cambs Regt
my
son and fellow craftsman
who fell in action at St Julien
31 July 1917
I dedicate this book

Introduction

'T HE old roads and their romances are the heritage of the modern tourist...Countless generations of men have built up the highways, the cities, towns, villages and hamlets along their course and have lived and loved, have laboured, fought and died through the centuries. Will you not halt awhile and listen to their story just as you may hap upon it. Every place has a story to tell for him to hear if he will. If he have no ears for such, so much the worse for him, and by so much the poorer his fairing.'

As I write I look through an arch covered with honeysuckle, and beyond a lilac bush in full flower to green fields and orchards of the 'highland' of the Isle of Ely. Between the garden and the green fields runs the road which provided the title of Charles Harper's book from which my quotation above is taken – the Cambridge, Ely & King's Lynn road. That road today carries traffic which has no time to study the lilac bloom, the apple blossom or the view across those green fields. The rise that takes these travellers on to the Island of Ely is no more than a slight incline which breaks the flatness of the fenland. They have no ears for the chiming of the church bells, no eyes for the village that they are bypassing with its 14th century cross and the mighty steam drainage engine which played such an important part in the draining of those flat acres through which the motorists speed.

It is here at home that I take refuge from what for many would be almost paradise – a room crammed from floor to ceiling with the thousands of books which form the Cambridgeshire Collection. The reader may feel that this is an 'out of the frying pan, into the fire' situation, as even here books climb the walls: but one cannot escape from them once the bug has bitten! These volumes however are different. These are mine, I have collected them myself, either because they relate to this area of the county – which to many will always be the Isle of Ely, never Cambridgeshire! – or because I have been able, in my professional capacity, to assist their author in some way. *Cambridgeshire Revisited* is not among them – yet.

But why should anyone interested in their county take refuge from what ought to be an idyllic working environment? Perhaps it is proof of self discipline: certainly in my younger days I would study those volumes till the library closed at 9 p.m. Now I finish by 6 p.m. daily, after only 8 hours in their company. Among other reasons for this flight is, perhaps, the lure of the countryside and its occupants.

If one examines the books about Cambridge itself one soon becomes aware that the town *per se* occupies far less space than the university to which it gives accommodation. The histories which have appeared over the past 200 years contain valuable chapters on the origin of the university and the history of the colleges, but little on the growth of Cambridge, the story of its theatres, trams, buses and railways.

Let us take a look at some of the more important volumes for the student of Cambridge history. Inevitably the name of Charles Henry Cooper must be foremost as, among his many works (which include histories of local villages including Cherry Hinton, Fen Ditton and Cottenham) two are pre-eminent. Published between 1842 and 1908, *Annals of Cambridge* is a five-volume chronological history of Cambridge based on corporation and other archives, supplemented in the later volumes with notes from the Cambridge newspapers. This monumental work is the basis for any study of Cambridge, although its chronological arrangement and style make it more fit for reference than for general reading. Some of the information presented in a more readable form is the basis of T. D. Atkinson's *Cambridge Described and Illustrated*, published in 1897. Cooper revised and supplemented Le Keux's *Memorials of Cambridge* to form virtually a new work, issued under his own name in 1860. J. J. Smith's *Cambridge Portfolio*, published in 1843, includes various items of interest, not least the illustrations by Ince, which include views of Petty Cury, Trinity St and Hobson's Conduit in 1838.

Of more recent date are the third volume of the *Victoria History of the County of Cambridge* which is devoted to Cambridge town and

University, although its coverage of the former is not comprehensive, and some sections, notably banking, are inaccurate. The three volumes on the City of Cambridge produced by the Royal Commission on Historical Monuments represent great value, both in content and price (at £5.25 they are the sole departure from my self-imposed 'non-Cambridge' collecting rule). Finally, there is the volume which most nearly corresponds with this present book – F. A. Keynes' *Byways of Cambridge History* originally published by Heffers, with chapters on Cambridge theatre, the Guildhall site and other topics of town history. *Cambridge Revisited* supplements these works with its chapters on the market hill fire of 1846, the Cambridge militia and the history of Green Street, and it, too, concentrates almost exclusively on the town.

Once the omissions in the published history of Cambridge can be identified then steps can be taken to remedy them. In recent years we have seen several such gap-fillers, among which can be numbered Alan Faulkner's *Fenland Barge Traffic* and *The Great Ouse* by D. Summers, which concentrate on the water-borne trade, *Cambridge Street Tramways*, by Sue Swingle, covering the 34-year history of that company, *The Cambridgeshire Landscape* by C. Taylor, with its section on the growth of the Barnwell area, and Enid Porter's *Cambridgeshire Customs and Folklore*, a monumental tribute to her dedication to the traditions of our county.

Then there are the books concentrating on other aspects – social conditions, housing, poetry and fiction, directories, church history, and books of illustrations. Included in this latter category are F. A. Reeve's *Victorian and Edwardian Cambridge from Old Photographs*, the volumes by Robert Farren, and W. B. Redfarn's *Old Cambridge*. If one considers the material published in the form of periodical articles, papers in the journals of local and national societies, etc, the reasons for seeking shelter in the country from this overwhelming wordage become more apparent!

Why then, in the face of all the available sources of information, should *Cambridge Revisited* be resurrected after 50 years? One reason is that it is in part a guidebook, and 'the old roads and their romances are the heritage of the modern tourist'. There have been many guidebooks, among the earliest of which was Thomas Salmon's *The Foreigner's*

Companion through the Universities of Cambridge and Oxford of 1748, which concentrated on the basic college round. Other guidebooks followed suit, some including illustrations and notes on town buildings, such as the castle and the Great Bridge. Once the railway arrived in 1845, with its capacity for transporting far more visitors than the slow, uncomfortable stage-coach, publishers were quick to recognise a new market and to produce guides providing a circular tour from the station. In desperation of university edifices to admire in the outer areas these guides were forced to pay some attention to town buildings. In modern times, however, guidebooks have tended to revert to the early emphasis on the university, and to rely almost exclusively on pictorial matter.

The first four chapters of *Cambridge Revisited* take the form of conducted walks away from the main tourist flow. They explore the side streets, pointing out little details which would otherwise go unnoticed: dates and initials scratched on a wall by troops stationed in Cambridge during the early days of the Great War, fragments of stone walls, unusual gravestones and cottages. An interesting guide to Cambridge streets for the resident or visitor, this book is also a step back into history, for these notes were written over 50 years ago. It is a fascinating exercise to follow in the author's footsteps today, discovering just what has survived 50 years of change, both in the city centre and along the streets off Newmarket Road. At the same time the reader will learn some of the history of the area, the reasons for the street names and a wealth of detail which brings the past to life.

This book is by no means a compilation of previously published facts; as the acknowledgements indicate, the author utilised the memories of an impressive number of experts and tapped the resources of the local history collections. This research has made *Cambridge Revisited* invaluable, the most popular section being the chapters on the Upware Republic and the Fen Ditton Penance which are constantly consulted by students. The illustrations include several by W. West whose series of views of Cambridgeshire villages made during the Great War are my particular favourites.

Recent years have seen a considerable growth of interest in local studies – during 1973 the Cambridgeshire Collection assisted some 3,600 students (another reason for escape to the country!), but there has been a dearth of interesting and readable books about the town of Cambridge which one could recommend to the general reader. *Cambridge Revisited* started life as a series of articles in Cambridge newspapers over 50 years ago. It was interesting then; the years have increased that interest. I am delighted that Patrick Stephens have decided to produce this reprint, and as proud to be associated with it as the Borough Librarian must have been with the original volume in 1921.

M. J. Petty ALA
Local Studies Librarian
Cambridgeshire Collection
Cambridgeshire Libraries
June 1974

Preface

IN the following pages no attempt has been made to tell once more the story of the University, Colleges and Town of Cambridge. Avoiding as far as possible the well-beaten track I have been content to wander amidst the bye-ways of local history, satisfied if I could penetrate to some small extent into the mass of curious and interesting lore which has gathered about Cambridge to an unusual degree.

These chapters, with two exceptions, were originally contributed to the *Cambridge Chronicle* (several appearing concurrently in the *Cambridge Daily News*). The friendly criticism, encouragement and offers of information which their appearance called forth came as an agreeable surprise to me, and, in consequence, I have been tempted to present them again to the public, after revision and with many additions, in a more permanent form.

But for the constant encouragement of Mr Ambrose Harding, who has advised and helped me with the book in all its stages, and whose support I cannot hope adequately to acknowledge, this little volume would never have been written.

To Mr A. T. Bartholomew I am also much indebted for reading these pages in manuscript and giving me valued direction. Mr A. H. Cook has added to the usefulness of the book by providing a good index, and has been indefatigable in clearing up difficult points of information.

I am under a great obligation to the Rev. Canon Bonney, Sc.D., F.R.S., who, drawing upon the memories of a long life, has specially written for these pages his personal reminiscences of Charles Kingsley, Professor E. H. Palmer, and of the Upware Republic Society.

Dr Courtney Kenny has permitted me to quote at considerable length from his article entitled *A Forgotten Cambridge Meeting-house*; and my thanks are also due to Mr R. F. Scott (Master of St John's College), Mr Arthur Gray (Master of Jesus College), Professor Sir William Ridgeway, Mr Francis Jenkinson (University Librarian), Sir Geoffrey Butler, Mr Bernhard Campkin, Mr W. A. Fenton (Borough Librarian), Mr Joseph Masters, Mr W. B. Redfern, Mr C. E. Sayle, the Rev. Dr. Stokes, my old friend Mr John Whitaker of Bridge Street, the Rev. J. F. Williams, the Rev. Canon E. G. Wood, the Rev. Evelyn Young and, last, but not least, to the anonymous donor of the Upware Republic Society's Visitors' Book referred to in Chapter X., which has thrown new light on an interesting aspect of University life in mid-Victorian times.

Turning now to the illustrations, I have to express my sincere thanks to Mr R. F. Scott (Master of St. John's College), for the use of the block showing St John's Street in 1863 ; and again to Mr Arthur Gray (Master of Jesus College), and to Miss E. Joyce Shillington Scales, the artist, for permission to reproduce the illustration of the Gateway on p. 65, and the typical Fen landscape seen on p. 137, which originally appeared in Mr Gray's *Tedious Brief Tales of Granta and Gramarye*. For the use of the woodcut of St Bene't's tower on the title-page I am indebted to the Syndics of the University Press ; the Council of the Cambridge Antiquarian Society most kindly placed at my disposal the fourteen half-tone blocks indicated by an asterisk in the list of illustrations ; and the Committee of the Cambridge Free Library allowed me to draw upon their interesting collection of local prints. The plans of mediaeval Cambridge and Stourbridge Fair are taken from *Life in Old Cambridge*, by the courtesy of the authoress, Miss M. E. Monckton Jones, and Mrs Bryan Walker has permitted me to reproduce Mr West's drawing of Chesterton Lane Corner made for her in 1911. Mr G. P. Hawkins allowed me to make use of his fine collection of Cambridge prints and playbills ; Mr Julian Julian (Borough Surveyor), spared no pains in assisting me to construct the plans of Green Street and of the detached portions of parishes in Newmarket Road ; Mr C. E. Brock, R.I., kindly presented me with the specially

drawn illustration reproduced on p. 49 ; Mr B. McLean Leach
gave me the sketch of the De la Pryme archway seen on p. 41 ;
and Mr T. P. Gallyon lent me three of the blocks illustrating
Chapter VII. Finally I have to acknowledge many charming
illustrations made by Mr W. West, and also others contributed by
Miss E. Fison, one of whose drawings is reproduced on the cover of
this volume.

Contents

List of Illustrations

    The illustrations marked with an asterisk are reproduced by kind permission of the
Council of the Cambridge Antiquarian Society.

The illustrations marked with an asterisk are reproduced by kind permission of the Council of the Cambridge Antiquarian Society.

LIST OF ILLUSTRATIONS

The illustrations marked with an asterisk are reproduced by kind permission of the Council of the Cambridge Antiquarian Society.

CHAPTER I.

Cambridge Revisited

I

THE title, *Cambridge Revisited*, which we have given to the following pages, has not been lightly chosen.

It implies a previous acquaintance with the principal objects of interest connected with the University and Town, and so should not deceive the new-comer, anxious to obtain such assistance as may be derived from more than one excellent guide-book to Cambridge.

It has, on the contrary, been our endeavour, even at the risk of descending occasionally to the trivial, to deal with matters not usually to be found in guide-books by giving the reader information either not readily accessible elsewhere, or which we have had the good fortune to bring to light for the first time.

With these few words of introduction and warning, we may now begin our first Walk through the town, choosing as a convenient starting point the western door of Great St Mary's Church.

We do not propose to trace in detail the history of this fine old Parish Church, but will content ourselves by remarking that it has had many vicissitudes, and has suffered much, at various times, from fire and neglect, alteration and restoration, and from the misdirected energies of fanatics and of purists in Gothic art. As recently as 1850 the late Sir Gilbert Scott swept away from the west end a quaint Italian portico, revealing in the process, behind the clock face of that time, the original plain dial, bearing the date 1679, which we see to-day.

The wrought iron railings with their decoration of Madonna lilies, enclosing the churchyard, are an excellent example of local craftsmanship, and before leaving we may glance at the tower-buttress immediately on the right of the western gates. Here will be seen a shallow circular depression cut into the stone, from the centre point of which is measured the mileage of the roads leading out of the town. From *Warren's Book* (Trinity Hall MS.)[1] we learn the date when the mark was cut :

> Oct. 19, 1732. A circular mark of 14 inches and an half in diameter, and about 2 foot 8 inches from ye ground, was cut on ye South-west Buttress of St Maries Steeple in Cambridge fronting the Publick Schools.
> From this Buttress ye sixteen miles from Cambridge to Barkway had before been measur'd.

On the opposite side of the road in the centre of Senate House lawn stands the huge bronze, known as the Warwick Vase, presented in 1842 by the Duke of Northumberland, then Chancellor of the University. It is a model of the original Greek marble vase which was found near Rome at the bottom of the lake at Hadrian's Villa, and which now stands in the grounds of Warwick Castle. The apparently substantial stone-like pedestal which supports this replica is but a clever mask in wood and paint of a mean though adequate support within !

The old walls and buildings of Cambridge have a flora of their own, and the botanist will note on or about the southern steps of the Senate House little tufts of Wall Rue (*Ruta muraria, L.*), the creeping tendrils of the Ivy-leaved Toadflax (*Linaria cymbalaria, Mill.*), and the Canadian Fleabane (*Erigeron canadensis, L.*). We have often watched with pleasure a picturesque figure in cap and gown bending affectionately over these jealously guarded little plants.

Directing our steps towards King's Parade and remarking the irregularities of architecture which its line of houses present to the opposing glories of King's Chapel, we soon arrive in front of the house numbered 11. Over the entrance, a neat red tablet records that " Charles Lamb lodged here in August, 1819." Here Lamb and his sister Mary met the little orphan daughter of Charles Isola, one of the Esquire Bedells of the University. They were afterwards to adopt her, and Lamb refers to her as " our Emma " in the letters of his later years.

[1] Ed. by A. W. W. Dale, Cambridge, 1911.

Until 1914 members of the well-known family of Deck for three
generations maintained (within the open space at the College entrance opposite, on New Year's Eve) the custom of firing out the
dying year, at the first stroke of midnight, by a rocket and, as the
vibration of the twelfth stroke ceased, of letting off another to

No. 5, BENE'T STREET, showing the rings under the eaves.

welcome in the New Year. The crowd that gathered to watch this
ceremony was gradually hushed to expectant silence as the clock's
hands crept towards the stroke of twelve, and broke out into loud
huzzas and mutual congratulations as the second rocket showered
overhead, and the bells of St Mary's burst out into a brief but
joyous peal.

Turning into Bene't Street, we notice, facing Free School Lane,
a picturesque seventeenth century house (No. 5), interesting from

the fact that under its eaves are to be seen three iron rings affixed to the roofplate. Rings of this sort were of great value in old times, when houses were of wood, and the destruction of burning buildings was the chief means of preventing the spread of fire. To the rings were fixed ropes or long firehooks for the purpose of pulling off the roof, and when man-power failed, teams of horses were brought in to help.

During our itinerary we shall notice several other houses where these curious appendages are obviously intended merely for ornament ; while sometimes the locality of the house suggests that the rings have been placed for the attachment of ropes giving temporary support to a hinged counter fixed to the tradesman's shop-front, upon which, on market-days, he might supplement the display of his wares.

Over the way stands St Bene't's Church, the oldest building in the town. From its Saxon tower, Hereward the Wake (*i.e.* the " awake " or the " watchful one ") may have gazed, using it as an observation post against the Normans. Note the long-and-short

FIREHOOK IN ST BENE'T'S CHURCH.

placing of its quoins, characteristic of Saxon work.[1] Within the
tower is one of the ancient firehooks just referred to, and it is on
record that this was last used in the Market Hill fire of 1849. Firehooks[2] used to be hung in convenient places on the outside of
buildings, and I am informed by Mr W. B. Redfern, whose pencil has
done so much to record old and vanished buildings in Cambridge,
that he well remembers this particular hook, complete with its
lengthy pole, hanging in its original position outside the west wall of
St Bene't's Church tower.

Turning back to Trumpington Street we hurry by the corner
house where from over the doorway a formidable stone monster
glares down upon us as he clasps to his side a bag inscribed £500,
and coming to Corpus Buildings, give a passing glance at the first
floor windows of No. 57, where Alfred Tennyson and his brother
Charles once occupied lodgings.

Opposite stands the Bull Hotel, the home, from 1784 until 1841,
of the famous Bull Book Club. It met weekly, and had a good
library of above 2,000 volumes. The number of members was
limited to fifty. At the Free Library may be seen a framed portrait-
group of the members with their names indicated. Amongst them
many well-known Cambridge family names occur, e.g. Robert
Bishop, James Bradwell, John Clay, James Gotobed, Richard
Hattersley, and Barnet Leach.

A Cambridge wit has explained that the Hotel was erected so
as to prevent Cats looking at Kings ! However this may be, the
main frontage and principal entrance of St Catharine's undoubtedly
" look at " Queens', and on approaching the former College from
Trumpington Street, through the pleasant little grove of elms, we
are apt to forget that, though its orientation has been changed,
we are entering by what was once the " back door."

St Catharine's was built to face Queens' Lane, because at the
time of Woodlark's Foundation (1473) that peaceful byway was of

---

[1] See woodcut.

[2] Cf. Sir William Davenant : " His hooke was such as heads the end of pole
                                    To pluck down house ere fire consumes it whole ; "
                                              Brittania Triumphans, 1637, p. 15.

considerable importance, and under the name of Milne, or Mill, Street led southwards to King's Mill, while its northern extremity survives as Trinity Hall Lane ; the intervening portion, long ago absorbed by the buildings and grounds of King's, is marked by Gibb's Buildings and the westernmost bay of the Chapel.

Between the court of St Catharine's and Trumpington Street, facing Corpus Christi College, once stood a considerable block of buildings, and it was only when this was cleared away that the Court was opened out and the elms planted, giving the agreeable prospect of greensward and ancient brickwork seen to-day.

A large portion of the cleared site was formerly covered by the extensive premises of the George Inn, the property of that worthy citizen and benefactor of Cambridge, Thomas Hobson. Here, where the College Chapel now stands, were the stables in which, as *The Spectator* tells us, were stalled the " forty good cattle " he let out for hire, and here was born that well-known saying, " Hobson's choice."

No. 68 Trumpington Street has an important place in the annals of the Perse School for Girls, for it was here, in 1881, that the School was launched on its career. Among the little band of sixteen scholars first enrolled was Mary Bateson, the distinguished historian.

Corpus Christi College has a special interest for Cambridge people, having been founded (1352) by the combined charity of the gilds of Corpus Christi and St Mary, two of the most famous of the town gilds.

It has been said that Cambridge lacks romance, nevertheless few of its colleges are without the dubious distinction of being haunted by a ghost, and probably the most notorious of these collegiate shades hangs about the Old Lodge of Corpus which, until recently, has been used as undergraduates' quarters. The story of its origin has many variants, but the generally accepted one runs as follows. Dr Butts, who held the office of Master of the College from 1626 to 1632 with conspicuous success, was Vice-Chancellor during the Plague of 1630, and seems to have dealt with the situation with the greatest ability and foresight.

Writing to Lord Keeper Coventry, High Steward of Cambridge, he gives a most pitiful account of the state of the town, and concludes :

. . . Myself am alone a destitute and forsaken man, not a Scholler with me in College, not a Scholler seen by me without. God all sufficient (I trust) is with me, to whose most holy protection I humbly commend your Lordship with all belonging unto you.

Undoubtedly his terrible experiences during the visitation preyed upon his mind, since, being about to preach before the University as Vice-Chancellor on Easter Day 1632, he was found hanging by his garters in his own chamber. His ghost is supposed to haunt the College.

According to another version the ghost is that of the unsuccessful suitor of the daughter of a later Master, Dr Spencer (1630-1693). Being interrupted during a clandestine interview, the unhappy lover, it is said, took refuge in a cupboard, still shown in the College Kitchen, where he died of suffocation.

In the *Occult Review* for March 1905, there is an article on the alleged phenomena, some of which are thus narrated :

In the Easter term of 1904, an undergraduate, . . . who had rooms opposite those said to be haunted, happened to come in at three o'clock in the afternoon, and as soon as he had sat down to do some work, found himself seized with a curious feeling of uneasiness, which made it impossible for him to concentrate his mind. He got up and, looking out of the window, noticed the head and shoulders of a man leaning out of a window of the upper set of rooms opposite. The features, he was rather surprised to find, he could not recognise : they were those of a stranger with long hair, who remained perfectly motionless, and seemed to glare down upon him. For three minutes he stood at the window and watched, and then, thinking he might see better from his bedroom, he ran there, but by the time he had arrived, the man opposite had completely disappeared. The young man was now thoroughly excited and went across the court to the upper set of rooms opposite. However, he found the door locked, and when he called no answer was given. In the evening, after careful enquiry he discovered that the owner of the rooms had been out the whole afternoon, and that it was quite impossible that anyone could have been in the rooms from the time of his departure at two o'clock to the arrival of his bedmaker at half-past six.

The troubles continuing, attempts to exorcise the spirit were made :

The occupant of the rooms made up his mind to try to exorcise it, and got C——, a friend from another College, who was interested in spiritualism, to come to his rooms for the purpose, with four other men.

At the outset they all knelt down, said the Lord's Prayer, and called upon the Three Persons of the Trinity to command the spirit to appear. It was then seen, but by only two of the six men. Another said that he felt a peculiarly cold and chilling air, but the rest saw nothing. The two who saw the ghost— the man interested in spiritualism and the occupant of the rooms—describe it as appearing in the form of a mist of about a yard wide, which slowly developed into the form of a man who seemed to be shrouded in white, and had a gash in his neck ; that it then moved slowly about the room. The two men got up, and, holding the crucifix in front of them, approached the apparition, but seemed to be forced back by some invisible agency. They cried out, " It drives me back," and then both completely broke down, becoming quite unnerved.

A few days later they tried again to exorcise the spirit, with exactly the same result : the same men saw it, and no one else. They were again driven back, although this time they approached holding hands. The others allege that they appeared to grow stiff, and that they gripped one another convulsively. The meeting was again broken up without anything definite having been effected.

The Old Court, however, has other interests, apart from occult phenomena. The windows on the ground floor of the west side, right in the corner where it meets the north side, mark the room in which Christopher Marlowe wrote his great play " Tambourlaine." Here again John Robinson (1576?-1625), pastor of the Pilgrim Fathers to America, once had rooms, as also Robert Browne (1550?-1633?), the originator of Brownists or Congregationalists.

Finally the old haunted Lodge once sheltered Matthew Parker (1504-1575), Master of the College and Archbishop of Canterbury, one of those " Cambridge Reformers," as they were called, who did so much to bring about the Reformation in England.

Continuing our walk southwards we soon arrive beneath the oriel window of Corpus, overlooking Trumpington Street, and nearest to St Botolph's Churchyard, and may see immediately below it the words " Henslow Common Informer " ; the last two words, however, can only now be read with difficulty. This fading record is an echo of the stormy days of politics in Cambridge during the election of 1825. The gross bribery and cruel cajolery then so rampant, found a strong opponent in Professor Henslow, who, for the bold stand he made, was thus pilloried by the party whose agents he so fearlessly exposed.

In St Botolph's Churchyard lies buried James Essex, a notable architect of the eighteenth century, and the last of the great Renaissance School, inaugurated by Inigo Jones and Wren. He was born and educated in Cambridge, his father being a well-known builder and craftsman in his day, who designed and built the elegant bookcases in the Catalogue Room of the University Library.

James studied architecture under Sir James Burrough, but began life, like his father, as a practical builder, executing amongst other works, the Mathematical Bridge at Queens' in this capacity, and not in that of architect.

Later, the "ingenious Mr Essex," as he is frequently called by his contemporaries, gradually drifted into the profession of architect, and received many important commissions in Cambridge and elsewhere, carrying out, amongst other notable works, the Dome Room at the University Library, the Ramsden Building at St Catharine's, the Cycloidal Bridge at Trinity, the West Front of Emmanuel, and the Georgian work at Madingley Hall.

He was also consulting architect at Ely, and superintended the much-needed restoration of the Lantern, and also at Lincoln, where he was responsible for the beautiful turrets and battlements of the central tower added after the collapse of the spire. Essex's last work for his native town was the erection of the Town Hall in 1782. To avoid confusion among the medley of buildings that are now collectively spoken of as the Town Hall, it will be well to note that what, at the present day, are known respectively as the " Small Room " and the " Vestibule " alone represent Essex's work, the building between this block and the Market Place being, of course, the Shirehall till 1842.

Essex was a friend and an executor of Cole the Antiquary, and built his house at Milton, which still exists. A letter written by Cole to him from Milton in 1779, contains the following quaint and pathetic request :

If I am underground at your Return (for I expect to go off suddenly and wish for it), as a Friend look at the spot, and as you contrived me a neat Place here for a temporary Dwelling, so I beg you . . . to ornament my longest home.

In later years he attained some distinction as an architectural historian, and wrote an interesting *Journal of a Tour through Flanders and France in* 1773.[1]

The railed-in tomb of the Essex family is on the south side of the chancel of St Botolph, and near by is a quaint stone structure, apparently covering a disused well.

The dedication of this church to St Botolph, the East Anglian patron Saint of travellers, serves to remind us of our close proximity to the ancient boundary of the town. It was the custom to place churches dedicated to St Botolph at the gates or without the walls of towns, in order to enable the traveller when setting out or returning, to place an oblation at his shrine and invoke protection, or proffer thanks as the case might be.

The limits and defences of mediaeval Cambridge were defined by the course of the river and of the King's Ditch. And here, where the Ditch, in its way from Mill Lane to Pembroke Street, crossed the road, stood the Trumpington Gates, through which Geoffrey Chaucer's two scholars doubtless passed when they made their memorable visit to the sturdy miller of Trumpington.

A glance at the sun-dials on the south-west buttress of the tower of St Botolph's, resplendent in their recent renovation of gilding, remind us that time is on the wing, so we will cross the road and hasten our steps to Peterhouse. On our way, we pass the picturesque Georgian building known now as Kenmare House, and in the eighteenth century as Randall House. This dwelling occupies the site of Cotton Hall which was sold in 1768 by one Pike, a wool-stapler of Bedford, to John Randall, Mus.Doc., a noteworthy organist of King's College Chapel, and Professor of Music.

---

[1] Ed. by W. M. Fawcett. Camb. Antiq. Soc., 8vo. publications No. **xxiv.** 1888.

Randall appears to have rebuilt the old Hall in the style of the period. The story goes that the University authorities asked that well-known character, Dr Jowett, of Trinity Hall, to inquire into the matter of chimes for the clock at Great St Mary's, and that

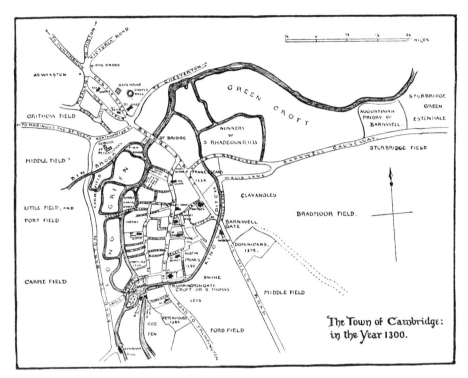

MEDIAEVAL CAMBRIDGE, showing Trumpington and Barnwell Gates.

he called to his aid a clever pupil of Dr Randall's, who, taking a suggestion from a few notes of Handel's, composed the celebrated Cambridge quarters, or chimes. The pupil proved to be no less a person than the famous Dr Crotch (1775-1847).

Before resuming our journey, we must note across the way the western façade of Pembroke Chapel, the earliest of Wren's works.

This building has an added interest, as being the first example of ecclesiastical architecture, free from Gothic influence, to be erected in England.

Leaving Kenmare House, we soon come to the church of St Mary the Less, with its singularly beautiful window-tracery, and raising our eyes to the adjoining wing of Peterhouse, note the iron bar which crosses an upper window looking into the eastern part of the churchyard. This bar marks the chambers of the poet Gray, and was introduced by him in 1756, for the purpose of hooking on a rope-ladder as a means of escape in case of fire. Gray's known terror of fire prompted the bucks of his college to play a cruel practical joke at the timid poet's expense ; for late one winter's night they placed a tub of water immediately beneath his window, and then raised a cry of fire on his staircase, whereupon he suddenly awoke, quickly hooked his rope-ladder to the iron bar and descended nimbly into the water awaiting him.

His resentment against the college authorities on failing to bring the culprits to book, decided Gray to transfer his residence to Pembroke, where, we are told, " he took care that his window should be always full of mignonette, or some other sweetly-scented plant," suggesting the thought that perhaps here we have the origin of the vogue for window-gardening, developing into the pretty custom by which Cambridge welcomed, with such floral profusion, her June visitors of a decade or so ago.

Facing Peterhouse stands the Master's Lodge, erected in 1701, and here the rings that we noticed under the eaves of the old house in Bene't Street, may be seen repeated on each of the four sides of the mansion. We may remark in passing that this is the only instance in Cambridge where the Master's residence is outside the college precincts.

A few yards further bring us to the Fitzwilliam Museum, where the lions, unlike Landseer's in Trafalgar Square, are posed in four different attitudes. Basevi was the architect of this beautiful building, of which he never saw the completion, for he was killed by stepping through a hole in some scaffolding in Ely Cathedral, while superintending the paintings on the roof of the nave.

We now cross the road to Fitzwilliam Hall, for a closer examination of the inscription appearing immediately above one of the ground floor windows, whose meaning seems somewhat obscure. The date 1727 is doubtless the year when this example of the architecture then in vogue was built, and the initials " I H " are probably those of the owner ; but of the cross and catherine wheel below them, nothing definite can be said, though by some it has been suggested that the catherine wheel perpetuates the name of an inn that once stood on this site.

Turning into Fitzwilliam Street, and passing down the left side, we come to a house (No. 22) having upon it a tablet inscribed :

CHARLES DARWIN
LIVED HERE IN
1836-7.

At the far end of the same street, at No. 13, once lived Charles Kingsley ; and Dr T. G. Bonney, of St John's College, who knew him well, has been kind enough to provide me with the following reminiscences of this great muscular Christian :

E. Fison

GROUND FLOOR WINDOW, FITZWILLIAM HALL,
showing date, initials, etc.

In May 1860 he was offered the Professorship of Modern History at Cambridge, and gave his inaugural lecture there on November 14th. The Prince of Wales (afterwards Edward VII.) resided for the terms of 1861, and Kingsley lectured to a class, of which he was a member, and took part in directing his studies, during which time Kingsley resided in Cambridge.   At the end of the year the Prince Consort died, and the Prince, after a journey to the East, married in 1863.   Kingsley then came up to Cambridge only for a part of the year, but continued to take an active part in University life ; being preacher in 1865 and having a great influence upon all the young men whom he met, from his frank cordiality and absence of " donnishness."   But he was even then beginning to wear himself out, as his " Life and Letters " shows ; and no wonder, for he threw himself heart and soul into whatever he was doing. One night, I remember, we went up, after a dinner in our Hall, to the rooms of another Devonian, and the two were telling stories, one against the other, in the Devon dialect to the delight of the rest.   Kingsley's slight stammer, which he had practically overcome in lecturing and preaching, was more perceptible in talk, and seemed to give effect to his remarks.   But, as I said, he was more delicate in health than he had been.   One bitter spring day I was walking along King's Parade, and met him coming in the opposite direction, with his shoulders up to his ears, and a picture of discomfort.   When met, he said, " What a miserable day ! "   " But, Professor," I replied, " it's a north-easter (see his poem in praise of the north-east wind).   " Ah, my d-d-dear fellow," he replied, " I was young and foolish then."   In his house at Eversley, he was the most delightful of hosts, and he was perhaps at his best when he retreated to his study in the later part of the evening.   Then he got into a South-American hammock, which he had slung from a beam, lighted a long clay pipe, and began to talk of natural history, theology, people he knew— whatever came uppermost.   His kindness and real courtesy to the humblest of his parishioners was not less remarkable than genuine.

In 1869 he resigned the Professorship, early in the year, and in August was appointed Canon of Chester, into which work he entered with his whole heart, stimulating the people to an interest in natural history.   In 1873 he was made a Canon of Westminster, visited America, after his duties there, lectured and travelled, wearing himself out still more, and returned to Eversley on August 18th.   Again, having with difficulty got through his work at the Abbey, and after returning to Eversley he broke down completely, and died of exhaustion on January 23rd, 1875.

Retracing our steps to Trumpington Street once more, we follow the course of the miniature silvery stream to the place where it bubbles up through a grating, marking the spot known, till the removal of the old Spital-Houses in 1852, as Spital-House End. Turning aside into Lensfield Road in order to examine the very flourishing ash in front of 2, Bene't Place, in whose trunk the iron railing is firmly embedded, we see a very good example of the vagaries of these trees. Crossing the road again on our way back we may pause awhile to gaze at Hobson's Conduit, and read the inscription telling us of its exile from the Market Hill. Such a quaint example of Jacobean work would have been a more fitting ornament to our Market Square than the present unsatisfactory erection.

Continuing our walk by the raised path alongside the water-course, we note on the other side of the road Sir Aston Webb's fine gateway to the Leys School, opened by King George V. on 30 April 1914. As we pass Brookside, we are reminded of some of its distinguished residents, the most eminent, perhaps, being Henry Fawcett, the blind Postmaster-General, whose funeral procession was watched by an enormous concourse of mourners lining almost the whole route of its long journey to the quiet churchyard at Trumpington.

Another resident was Charles Cardale Babington, Professor of Botany, author of a *Flora of Cambridgeshire.* The name of this distinguished botanist recalls the introduction into England of the Canadian water-weed (*Anacharis alsinastrum,* Bab.) in which he was greatly interested. This plant had already accidentally found its way into England from North America, but was unknown in Cambridge until 1848.[1] Originally placed in this little stream by the Curator of the Botanic Garden, it passed through the outlet into Vicar's Brook and thence to the river, where its prodigious fertility soon became a source of no little inconvenience to navigation, and eventually caused it to spread far beyond the limits of the Fens. Happily, it has now largely disappeared from the river, its vitality has long been waning, and it is no longer a serious and costly pest.

Arriving before the entrance of the Botanic Garden, let us note that the handsome gates which were re-erected here in May, 1909, originally served as the entrance-gates to the old Physic Garden in Downing Street, on the site now partly occupied by the new Laboratories. Entering the gates and turning immediately to the right, near the brook may be found a lime tree with a tablet at its

[1] Miller and Skertchly, *The Fenland,* 1878, p. 307, *et seq.*

base, recording that this tree was planted by Dr Tatham, Vice-Chancellor, on the occasion of the foundation of the Garden, 9 November 1846. It is not often that one has the data for estimating correctly the age of an adult forest tree : the only other fully-grown dated specimens in the district known to us being the fine Oriental plane in the Fellows' Garden at Jesus, planted by Professor Edward Daniel Clarke in 1802 ; the limes in the Avenue of Trinity, laid out

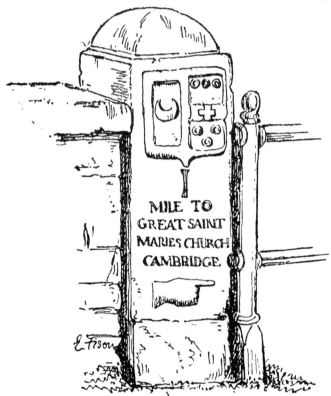

MILE TO
GREAT SAINT
MARIES CHURCH
CAMBRIDGE

THE FIRST MILESTONE.

in 1672 ; and the famous plane in the Palace garden at Ely, planted by Bishop Gunning (1614-1684) more than two hundred years ago.

Proceeding a few steps further along the main road we find buttressed against Trumpington Stone-bridge (a corruption of

FIREHOOK IN USE,
from an old print entitled *The Thatch-hook*, 1620.

E. P. PHELPS. DEL.

ST BENE'T'S TOWER

Face page 16

Milestone-bridge), the first milestone out of Cambridge, conspicuous on account of its size, and by the coat of arms carved upon it, intended to represent the arms of Trinity Hall impaling those of Dr Mowse, a former Master (*viz.* Or, on a Fess, between 3 Annulets in Chief and as many in Base, (2 and 1) Sable, a Cross patée of the Field).

This stone was erected, on the occasion of the visit of George II. to the University in 1728, in place of the original and smaller one, the first of sixteen milestones, set up between Cambridge and Barkway in the early part of the eighteenth century and paid for out of funds left to Trinity Hall by Dr Mowse (Mouse, or Moss, died 1588) and his friend and executor, a certain Mr Hare. To commemorate the source of the " Causey-money " so used, the arms of the second of these benefactors were placed on the last stone at Barkway, and those of Dr Mowse on the one before us.

And now, since Dr Crotch's chiming quarters remind us that our hour, as well our first mile is ended, we may fitly conclude our first expedition.

CHAPTER II.

Cambridge Revisited

2

OR our second Walk, No. 1 Trinity Street is another good starting-point. In the publishing world, No. 1 Trinity Street will always be of interest on account of its long association with the great house of Macmillan; for although it was at No. 17, in 1843, that this now world-renowned business first saw the light, it moved two years later to these corner premises.

The section of the roadway between here and the Senate House, known as the Senate Hill, arouses the very natural enquiry as to the fitness of the term " hill " for so level a space. We must remember, however, that the disappearance of the once relatively higher ground both here, and at Market Hill, Peas Hill, and St Andrew's Hill, is due to the gradual levelling up of the lower and consequently swampy portions, in order to secure sufficiently firm foundations for the buildings of the growing town; and though it has taken many centuries to obliterate the original contour, it is interesting to find these ancient features perpetuated by their old place-names.

Pondering upon this vista of years, we will cross the Hill and go down Senate House Passage to Trinity Hall Lane, in quest of " Jowett's Little Garden." Following the narrow lane for a few paces to the left and turning a corner we find ourselves facing one of the most picturesque groups of buildings Cambridge has to show, and here, railed off from the street, and enclosed in an angle of the wall of Trinity Hall, is a diminutive piece of ground supporting a few shrubs—the " little garden " we have come to see !

Fame has not been kind to Joseph Jowett, LL.D. (1752-1813), Master of Trinity Hall. This worthy man came of a Leeds family and made no small reputation in his day. But now all his good works are forgotten, save the trivial one before us, and this has made its creator immortal among Cambridge men by reason of the following epigram :

> A little garden little Jowett made
> And fenced it with a little palisade :
> But when this little garden made a little talk,
> He changed it to a little gravel walk ;
> If you would know the mind of little Jowett
> This little garden doth a little show it.[1]

This little garden of Jowett's serves to mark the neighbourhood of the original entrance to the College, which existed until 1873, when the old gateway was removed and re-erected as an entrance from Garret Hostel Lane. Passing down a narrow passage a few yards further on, between Trinity Hall and the Chapel of Clare, we find, some fifty yards from the entrance and incorporated in the modern brickwork forming the boundary of Trinity Hall, a section of ancient wall composed of rubble and clunch.

This early fragment of stone once formed part of the mediaeval Hostel founded by Prior Crawden, about 1340, for the free accommodation of a limited number of such monks of Ely as desired to avail themselves of a University education. When, a few years later, William Bateman, Bishop of Norwich, purchased the building in order to add it to his Foundation of Trinity Hall, the Ely monks removed to Burden's (or Borden's) House, at the south-west corner of Green Street.

Retracing our steps in the direction of Garret Hostel Lane, let us make a brief pause before the ivy-mantled garden wall of Caius, spiked with gay antirrhinums, when a glance at its brickwork, about two feet from the pavement level, near the Lecture Room will reveal a small oblong wooden shutter covering an opening in the wall, a simple contrivance for enabling the college fire-hose to be connected quickly with the adjacent street hydrant in case of an outbreak of fire.

[1] There are many versions of these lines, which are usually attributed to Porson.

Turning into Garret Hostel Lane, the last of the many little lanes which once lead down to the river, we pass on our way the age-scarred wall of clunch dating back to 1545, and noting the marble boundary-tablet recently affixed at its end, soon find ourselves standing before the old but re-erected gateway of Trinity Hall already referred to.

It was at the time of the rebuilding of Garret Hostel Bridge in 1837 that the slipway between Trinity Hall and the bridge approach was enclosed by the College authorities, an act arousing no little resentment among the townsfolk, who vented their rage by smashing off every one of the spearheads that once graced the iron railings, which still remain in their mutilated state to bear witness to the folly of man.

The present iron bridge replaces an old wooden structure known as the mathematical bridge, erected by Essex in 1769. As will be seen from the frontispiece, its timber-work in some respects resembles that of the present mathematical bridge of Queens', also built by Essex (1750) from a design by a Mr Etheridge. In the summer of 1812, Garret Hostel bridge broke down, its restoration being undertaken at the joint expense of the town and Trinity Hall.

The views from this spot vie with any of the lovely vistas that Cambridge can present. Seen on some sunny day in early June, the Cam, flowing beneath many bridges and weeping willows, between trim gardens and broad lawns, beside stately avenues and old buildings half hidden by summer verdure, recalls Spenser's description of a similar scene :

> And in the midst a little river play'd
> . . . .
> Beside the same a dainty place there lay,
> Planted with myrtle trees and laurels green,
> In which the birds sung many a lovely lay."[1]

Down stream lies " that long walk of limes," referred to in *In Memoriam*, interrupted by the bridge with three cycloidal arches built by Essex. On the other side, to the south, we can dimly discern from where we are standing two stone shields embedded in

---

[1] *Faerie Queene*, III., c. V., 39-40.

the terrace-wall of Trinity Hall. These two carved stones were removed to their present position from an old summer-house that stood over the river at the foot of the north walk in the Fellows' Garden. They can be seen on the outside wall of this house in Loggan's view (1688). The summer house was pulled down in 1708.

A short detour by Clare Hall Pieces will enable us to observe the old worn mounting steps beside the road directly opposite the entrance to Clare Avenue. These steps, a remnant of the old coaching days, were set up by the College authorities for the greater convenience of their servants when handling the students' luggage : it will be readily appreciated that the restricted roadway at the College's front gate would not have permitted the approach and return of a four-in-hand.

Directing our attention to King's meadow, we notice two hillocks surrounded by elms, the relics of an avenue raised on a high causeway that formerly served as an approach from Clare Hall Pieces to the old bridge of King's, whose two arches, till 1819, spanned the river opposite the fine portico of Gibb's building.

The wooden railings once fencing off Clare Hall Pieces from the road, disappeared for ever in the flames of the great bonfire lit on Market Hill in honour of the late Lord Kitchener's visit to Cambridge in 1898.

Making our way back to Garret Hostel Bridge and looking thence towards Trinity, above the wall skirting the slipway to the river, we see, amidst a mass of foliage and ivy, the lofty and now disused Brewhouse of the College, with the adjoining roof of the former residence of the brewer,[1] one of whose daughters lies buried in the Mill Road Cemetery, her tombstone recording that she was " born in Trinity College."

As seen from the riverside, these ivy-mantled buildings form, with the adjoining wall of Garret Hostel Lane, a picturesque and romantic corner. Here, at the proper season, boats for hire attract a gay and lively crowd, and here the curious observer penetrating into the deeper shade finds embedded in the walls, four great stone

[1] As we go to press comes the news that these picturesque buildings are soon to be demolished.

The Brewery Corner, Trinity College.

W. West.

shields of arms, framed in renaissance scrollwork, which impart an air of mystery to the scene. The first shield nearest the river, shows the arms of Sir Thomas Sclater, Bart., another bears the quartered arms of Babington, whilst the remaining two repeat the saltire of Nevile.

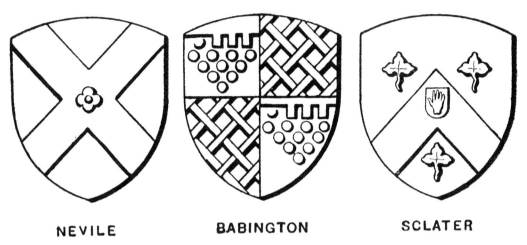

NEVILE   BABINGTON   SCLATER

ARMS FROM THE BREWERY CORNER.

The well-known Dr Thomas Nevile, Master of Trinity (1593-1615) and Dean, successively, of Peterborough and Canterbury, built, at his own expense, the greater part of Nevile's Court, and when, later, Wren's great Library was built at its western end, it was placed at such a distance as to necessitate the prolongation of the cloisters on either side by the addition of four arches to each.

The northern extension, by four arches, was undertaken by Sir Thomas Sclater, a former Fellow, whilst Dr Humphrey Babington (1615-1691), Vice-Master, undertook the extension, also by four corresponding arches, on the opposite side. The connection between the original and the later work on the northern and on the southern sides of the Court was marked by two stone shields, bearing the arms, respectively, of Dr Nevile and of the benefactor on whose building it was placed.

In later years the work of Sclater and of Babington was found to be unsafe ; the "ingenious" Mr Essex was called in as architect, "restoration" took place, the Court assumed its present form, and the shields of our three benefactors found a last resting place in the brewery corner.

Whilst retracing our steps towards Trinity Street by way of the New Court, and Trinity Lane, we are reminded, as we cross the Avenue, of the now obsolete conundrum : "Why is the Trinity Avenue like a Trinity Fellowship ? " the answer being, " Because both are limited to a narrow view ending in a church." Formerly the spire of Coton Church could be discerned at the far end of this long vista of foliage.

ARMS OF BABINGTON.

Passing through the New Court, where the meretricious stuccoed buildings with their painted cast iron mullions need not detain us, we soon find ourselves before Nevile's Gate and remarking its quaint Jacobean pediment proceed to recall its many vicissitudes. Originally the entrance gate to the western approach of Nevile's Court, it ceased to serve its purpose upon the extension of the cloisters, and, in 1680, was re-erected at the end of the Avenue, only to be replaced in 1733 by the present handsome iron gates from Horseheath. The old Gate was then removed to the stable yard entrance at the corner of Garret Hostel Lane, and in 1876 it was once more removed and finally re-erected in its present position.

Leaving the Gate we will now scrutinise that portion of Trinity wall beneath the first chimney-stack, when, between the two upper windows and a little below the line of level of their sills, we shall discover the fragment of an ancient iron hold-fast, the sole survivor of others that once held a notice-board cautioning vagabonds, evil-doers and such-like gentry, to be upon good behaviour whilst in the town ; an old inhabitant well recollects seeing this board and reading the drastic nature of the punishment threatening those who failed to respect its injunctions.

Proceeding towards Trinity Street, we pass, some few yards before reaching that thoroughfare, the modern Trinity Lecture Room, built of white brick upon the site where, until 1864, stood the ancient Ely Almshouses, those three quaint tenements still remembered by an older generation on account of their old-fashioned hatch-doors and the fine panelling of their rooms.

These houses were built about the year 1473, out of funds left for the purpose by Reginald Ely, a well-known freemason of Cambridge, who was one of the builders of King's College in 1444 when, (Dr Venn tells us), he had a license to impress workmen for the purpose. Caius College subsequently became trustees of the property, and on the site being sold in 1864, to Trinity, erected the present pleasant dwellings in St Paul's Road.

Entering Trinity Street we face St Michael's and, making our way into this interesting Decorated Church, we shall find a life-size portrait of King Charles I. hanging on the east wall of the north aisle. The painting shows some of the emblems seen in the frontis-piece to *Eikon Basilike* (1689), viz. a storm-beaten rock, the royal crown lying at the King's feet, and in his hand a circlet of thorns ; exemplified by the following verses :

> And as th' unmovéd Rock out-brave's
> The boist'rous Windes and rageing waves
>
> So triumph I. And shine more bright
> In sad Affliction's Darksom night,
>
> That Splendid, but yet toilsom Crown
> Regardlessly I trample down.
>
> With joie I take this Crown of Thorn
> Though sharp, yet easie to be born.

Returning to the street, let us resume our walk in the direction of St John's. The eye is soon arrested by the elaborate pargetting of that fine example of a timber house of the 16th century, for many years before 1893 occupied by Messrs. Foster's Bank, and for many generations remarkable as being the scene of continuous and bustling activity. It is curious to note that its present use as a rendezvous for the partaking of our truly national institution "Afternoon Tea," re-echoes and forms a connecting link with Cambridge life in the 17th century, when these same premises figured as a well-known Coffee House under the name of the Turk's Head, where undergraduates flocked for refreshment and gossip, and perusal of the news-letters and newspapers of that time.

THE TURK'S HEAD COFFEE HOUSE (now Matthew's Café), reproduced from W. B. Redfern's *Old Cambridge*, 1876.

When the celebrated Dr John North, sometime Master of Trinity and Clerk of the Closet to Charles II., was an undergraduate, we are told by his biographer, Roger North, that he behaved with exemplary piety and decorum. "Coffee houses being but young." Very soon, however, matters grew worse, and Coffee houses more attractive, and our author remarks, more in sorrow than in anger: "that it is become a custom, after Chapel, to repair to one . . . where hours are spent in talking . . . which is a vast loss of time grown out of a pure novelty, for who can apply close to a subject with his head full of the din of a Coffee house ? "

Opposite to the Café stands the red brick Georgian house (No. 32), for many years (1791-1813) the residence and business premises of John Bowtell, book-binder, antiquary, and philanthropist.

Bookbinding has been a craft of no little importance in Cambridge since the end of the 15th century, and Bowtell was one of the last representatives of a class of tradesmen now extinct, namely the Cambridge Stationers, who not only sold stationery, prints, and books, but were practical printers and bookbinders as well. He acquired a considerable fortune and left a large sum to Addenbrooke's Hospital, where his portrait may be seen ; and Dyer, in his *Privileges*, gives some interesting gossip about him and his *History of the Town*, from which I extract the following passages :

On his first coming to town (as I am informed by his nephew, Mr Bowtell, of Cambridge, who succeeds him in business), Mr B. received a little tuition from a gentleman of St John's College, and gained a tolerable knowledge of the Latin and French languages, and I think a little Greek. He was fond of general reading, but more particularly of topographical ; and, as many curious works of this kind presented themselves to him in the way of his business, his rule was, first to read them, and to make extracts, and then to bind them ; and thus, book-reading and book-binding doing, very laudably, their separate business, Mr Bowtell acquired at the same time, considerable knowledge and very handsome property.

It was natural, with his peculiar taste, that Mr B.'s curiosity should be directed to the history of the town, in which he resided, more particularly when such opportunities were every day occurring to gratify it. He not only read and extracted much in the way above-mentioned, but became personally active and externally inquisitive, by examining parish registers, and every sort of public instrument which fell in his way, that could throw light on the History of the Town.

Mr B. having thus collected a great variety of materials, formed it into a regular History. . . . The author was engaged on it, I understand, for 18 years.

The manuscript of this laborious work still lies unpublished in the library of Downing College.

It will be noticed that the two new houses, Nos. 28 and 27, have iron rings under their eaves similar to those seen upon the old house in Bene't Street, thus supporting our suggestion that, in later days, these rings were only intended by the architect to serve a decorative purpose.

Passing the corner premises, known to undergraduates, on account of the sumptuous apartments within, as the " Ritz," we come to Trinity Great Gate, and note the public water supply at the foot of the south tower, whose never-failing service householders even now find convenient. It may not be generally known that its source lies in a field near the Madingley Road, a little beyond the Observatory approach, and that its conduit pipe crosses the river bend opposite the north end of Trinity Library. The conduit pipe appears originally to have been carried much further to the east, causing Sidney Street to be known as Conduit Street in early days, before the foundation of the College from which it takes its present name.

As we pass the east end of Trinity Chapel we note the date of its completion, 1564, inscribed above the window. For those who are interested in coincidences we may recall the fact that this year saw also the birth of Shakespeare, who died in 1616, on the same day that Cromwell entered Sidney College as a student.

Turning into the kitchen lane of St John's, a few yards bring us to a large first floor window on the right hand side, immediately above the beginning of the covered portion of the lane. This window marks the rooms once occupied by Wordsworth, and bears a stained glass inscription recording this fact. These quarters are commemorated by Wordsworth himself in the following well-known passage from the *Prelude* :

> The Evangelist St John my patron was :
> Three Gothic courts are his, and in the first
> Was my abiding-place, a nook obscure ;
> Right underneath, the College Kitchens made
> A humming sound, less tuneable than bees,
> But hardly less industrious ; with shrill notes
> Of sharp command and scolding intermixed.
>
> . . . .
>
> And from my pillow, looking forth by light
> Of moon or favouring stars, I could behold
> The antechapel where the statue stood
> Of Newton with his prism and silent face,
> The marble index of a mind for ever
> Voyaging through strange seas of thought alone.

TRINITY STREET (1855), showing old All Saints' Church.

Face page 28

The tragic death of Rupert Brooke is still fresh in our minds, and the memorial cross on the other side of the road, marking the site of old All Saints' Church, recalls the memory of Henry Kirke White (1785-1806), yet another Cambridge poet prematurely cut off in the flower of youth.

White, who was the son of a butcher at Nottingham, showed signs of literary tastes at an early period in his brief though romantic and melancholy career. His ambition to come to Cambridge prompted him to write *Clifton Grove* with a view to raising the necessary funds, but it was not a financial success. Charles Simeon, however, and other friends interested themselves in the young poetaster and secured for him a sizarship at St John's in 1805, but his health, which had already showed signs of weakness, was quickly broken down by too close application to study, consumption developed, and, in the following October (1806) White died in his college rooms in the twenty-second year of his age, and was buried in the chancel of the old church. In 1819 a tablet to his memory, with a medallion by Chantrey and an inscription by Professor William Smyth was placed above his grave at the expense of a young American admirer, Francis Boott, of Boston.

Churches are not often sold by auction, but old All Saints' came beneath the hammer and was demolished in 1865, leaving a plain flagstone to mark the last resting place of White, whom misfortune seemed to have pursued, even into the tomb.

> See, as the prettiest graves will do in time,
> Our poet's wants the freshness of its prime!

Subsequently, a new and greater All Saints' Church rose upon a site immediately opposite the entrance to Jesus College, and was duly christened " St Opposites " by the irreverent undergraduates of the time. Meanwhile, Chantrey's medallion was removed by one of the churchwardens pending a decision as to its future home. After an undignified interregnum of five years, a faculty was granted in 1870, by the Bishop, in response to a petition from the parishioners that it might be placed in St John's Chapel. Here it may now be seen under the west window, together with a brass tablet recording its history.

Time has judged Southey as having much over-rated White's verse, nevertheless Byron in 1809 wrote sympathetically of his memory in the following lines :

> Unhappy White ! while life was in its Spring
> And thy young muse just shook her joyous wing,
> The Spoiler came : and all thy promise fair,
> Has sought the grave, to sleep for ever there.

It may not generally be known that the theme of the stirring hymn " Oft in danger, oft in woe " (No. 291, *Hymns A. and M.*), originated with White, and it is interesting too, to trace its curious vicissitudes ; the opening line as it left White's pen read " Much in sorrow, oft in woe " ; in 1827, we find a little maiden of fourteen, by name Frances Fuller-Maitland, re-writing and enlarging it ; and, passing through the hands of other revisers, it finally appeared in 1836 in its present familiar form.

With the autumn of 1906, the centenary of White's death, came a request from across the Atlantic that a wreath might be placed upon his grave, showing that Fame had not entirely deserted one of Cambridge's lesser poets.

Resuming our walk once more, a few steps beyond St John's Chapel, we notice looking westwards across the street, a cluster of old out-buildings, quaint gables and quainter chimney-stacks and, peeping above them all, the spire of St Clement's, a medley of centuries' encrusted brick and tile presenting a charming silhouette against the evening sky.

Whilst we are upon the subject of old houses, it is worth re-membering that behind many of the plain façades that line our streets lie shaded courts, mud-walled cottages, thatched roofs, plots of grass, and trees, relics of peaceful rural surroundings, now gradually being swallowed up and obliterated by the ever growing town.

If we would emulate the immortal Doctor Syntax in search of the picturesque, we cannot do better than continue our journey to Park Street, by way of Round Church Street, where, a few paces to our left will bring us to St Clement's Place. We enter through its covered approach, and find ourselves in the cloistered stillness of its

St John's Street, about 1863.

SEPULCHRAL SLAB IN ST CLEMENT'S CHURCHYARD.

Face page 31

court, to which the old white thatched cottage at its end imparts a pleasant air of rusticity.   Another relic of country life is the large thatched barn in the yard adjoining 36, King Street.

From St Clement's Place to St Clement's Church, by way of Portugal Place, is but a short distance, and here, within the angle formed by the eastern boundary of the churchyard and the adjoining railings, we may see, resting against the old scarred wall, a curious looking tombstone depicting a gruesome figure of Death, holding in one hand an hour-glass, and in the other a spear.

Much might be written concerning sepulchral slabs, of which this sermon in stone, with its sombre message, is an interesting example.   But the carved hour-glass, upheld in the effigy's bony grasp, reminds us that time is fleeting.   We have loitered too long by the wayside, and must awake, once more to mundane things. And so we leave this quiet resting-place and, praying that we may long escape Death's inevitable spear, make our way along the passage to the busy street beyond.

CHAPTER III.

Cambridge Revisited

3

WE cannot do better than begin our third Walk through the town at Hyde Park Corner, by the tall spire of the Roman Catholic Church. The name of the foundress of this richly decorated building is recorded in an inscription above the transept window facing the street, and the fortune which made its erection possible is said to have been derived from the manufacture of movable eyes for dolls, a fact which led a frivolous Protestant, more careful of wit than of truth, to declare that this costly pile was "built out of dolls' eyes to contain i-dols."[1]

Here, at the cross-roads, stood one of the more important of the Cambridge wayside Crosses.[2] "Dawe's Cross," for such was its name, appears to have been a conspicuous landmark from the crude pictures of it which remain, and its approximate site is now permanently and appropriately marked by the fine church we have just referred to.

Opposite the church stand the modern buildings of the Perse School. It was in the spring of 1891 that the School removed to this spot from its old quarters in Free School Lane. This ancient Foundation of Dr Perse (1615) includes in its long Roll of scholars the names of Jeremy Taylor (1613-1667) and of Edward Henry Palmer (1840-1882), the Orientalist. To Dr T. G. Bonney I am

[1] E. M. Forster, *The Longest Journey*, 1907.
[2] Cf. Dr Stokes, *C. A. S. Proc.*, Vol. xx

indebted for the following biographical sketch of Palmer, with whom he was well acquainted :

Edward Henry Palmer, born in Green Street, Cambridge, where his father had a school, on August 7th, 1840, was left an orphan at a very early age, and brought up by an Aunt, as if he were her own child. He was delicate, inheriting a tendency to bronchial asthma, but with some muscular strength and much coolness in danger. Educated at the Perse School, he went, when about 16 years old to a house of business in London, but had already got a knowledge of Romany from talking to gypsies near Cambridge. In London he picked up Italian and French in the same colloquial way, but his health broke down and he came back to Cambridge, as doctors feared, to die, in 1859. But after a strange crisis, produced by a dose of *Lobelia*, he recovered, and began learning Oriental languages, having found a teacher in a native of India, one Syed Abdullah, then resident in Cambridge. He made rapid advances, became known to C. J. Newbery, and A. H. Calvert, and through them to J. Todhunter, all Fellows of St John's, and by their advice joined the College as a sizar. He read enough Classics to obtain a place in the third class of the Tripos, but his time was mainly devoted to Oriental languages, in which his reputation rapidly increased. He was elected first a Scholar, then a Fellow. In the early part of 1869 he was appointed one of the members of the party, headed by Captain Wilson, for surveying the peninsula of Sinai, to which his knowledge of vernacular Arabic made his services of the highest value. Returning for a short time to England in the summer of 1869 Palmer went out again in a few months to explore the great limestone upland, north of Sinai, and south of Palestine proper, the Tîh or Wilderness of the Wandering. On this adventurous journey he was accompanied by Mr Charles Tyrwhitt Drake, of Trinity, whom weak health had driven to more genial climates. They had no dragoman and little baggage, and made their way, hiring camels as they went, first to Sinai (where they obtained important literary results) drawing maps, and collecting all possible information, hunting especially for inscribed stones and Biblical places. They ultimately arrived at Jerusalem in May, 1870. Here Palmer and Drake stayed some time, investigating the topography of the former Temple area, and the question of the date of the Dome of the Rock. Then he went northward, over more familiar ground, and returned to England in the autumn of 1870.

In 1871 the Professorship of Arabic fell vacant. Palmer stood for it, but was not elected, and though a man of merit was preferred, circumstances in the election made the result peculiarly mortifying. The electors were the Heads of Houses ; men, at that time, on whom knowledge of the unusual dawned slowly, and who were afraid of the unconventional. That Palmer certainly was, even in his amusements—conjuror, an adept at all tricks of sleight of hand, mesmerist, about his only outdoor pleasure was a day's fishing in the fens. Report says that coming to College one evening from the river, very wet and dirty, he met Dr Bateson, then Master, who enquired : " Is that Eastern costume, Professor ? " " No, Master," was the prompt reply, " Eastern counties."

Late in 1871, the Lord Almoner's Professorship of Arabic also fell vacant, and Gerald Wellesley, Dean of Windsor, offered it to Palmer. It was a poor thing, worth about £40 a year, but it had the advantage that he could marry without losing his fellowship. That, as he had been for some time engaged, he promptly did, and began to give lectures in Arabic and Persian in March, 1872. Next year, when the Oriental Languages Tripos was instituted the University added £250 a year, but here again they drove a harder bargain with Palmer than with Dr Wright, the Professor of Arabic. But yet more serious trouble was coming. After the birth of two children (girls) Mrs Palmer's health failed about 1876, and she had to live at Bournemouth and on the Continent till her death in the summer of 1878. His finances were overburdened, though he worked incessantly, writing for Indian newspapers, and many valuable books in English, besides work of a lighter and more remunerative character.

In the summer of 1879 he married again, gave up his extra work and pay in Cambridge, and settled in London. But in the spring of 1880 Arabi's rebellion broke out. Palmer was consulted by the English Government, for an attack by his (Arabi's) supporters on the Suez Canal was feared, and then a general rising of the Arabs on the Eastern side of it. The position was very critical, and Palmer thought it his duty to go to Egypt. He went, arrived in Egypt in July, 1881, disappeared into the desert, saw the most powerful Sheiks, made the Canal safe, and won them over to the English cause, and got back to Suez in the beginning of August, and then on the 9th, with Captain Gill and Lieut. Charrington and a European servant, went back with money which he had promised to the Sheiks. To save time he passed through a tribe not yet known to him. Here treachery led to the capture of the party. They were driven, almost unclothed, to the edge of a ravine, placed in a row there, and shot on the morning of August 12th. The chief traitor died soon of fear and remorse, justice was dealt out to those who had aided him, and some time afterwards the relics of these brave men were collected and entombed in the vaults of St Paul's, near the graves of Wellington and Nelson."

Let us now direct our steps towards Parker's Piece. This delightful playground of Cambridge was acquired by the Town in 1613, in exchange for the ground which now forms the paddocks of Trinity College, and takes its name from one Edward Parker who held a lease of the property at the time of the transaction. Before Fenner's was opened in 1846, all the University and County cricket matches were played on Parker's Piece and, as prints of the period show, the players wore tall hats. The County of Cambridge

PARKER'S PIECE IN 1842

showing the old Borough Gaol and, among the
poplars on the west, the Windmill from which
Mill Road takes its name.

CORONATION DINNER, 1838.

Face page 35

has an honourable place in cricket annals, and is thus referred to in Daft's *Kings of Cricket*, 1893 :

Cambridgeshire was for many years as good a county as any, as well it might be, having two such champion batsmen as Hayward and Carpenter, and such a bowler as G. Tarrant. It possessed an excellent little player, too, in Jack Smith, who was a fine batsman and as good an out-field as I ever saw. Duckey Diver was another of its best men, and Dan Hayward, a brother of Tom, was a very useful player. These men, as it was afterwards proved, were destined, with the aid of one or two more, to raise the county of Cambridgeshire to almost as high a position as that now occupied by Surrey.

Of the many national rejoicings that Parker's Piece has witnessed none stands out so pre-eminently as the Coronation Festival of 1838, when 15,000 people were seated to a substantial dinner in the open air. Many times have many writers told the story of this truly gargantuan feast, and of the immense quantity of provisions consumed. On sixty tables were distributed, besides other substantial fare, 1,608 plum puddings of about 6½lbs. each.

No reference to Parker's Piece would be complete without mention of the hustings, that storm-centre of political faction erected on the part of the Piece lying towards Clarendon Street. Here the rival candidates addressed the " free and independent voters of the ancient Borough of Cambridge," and here too our fathers mounted the wooden steps and publicly recorded their votes, to the din of cheers and booings from the watching crowd below.

Many good stories are told by the passing generation of these lively times ; of the hefty form of Orator Bell, with his twenty stone of " too too solid flesh " tightly wedged in his donkey-chaise, and of the hugeness of his blue and buff favour. Suffice it to say that the processions and chairings to the " Hoop " or the " Eagle " were conducted in the true Eatanswill style, and with all the accompanying incidents as witnessed on a certain memorable day by our friend Mr Pickwick.

The flourishing row of limes fronting Parkside was planted in 1867, at the suggestion and expense of the late Mr J. Odell Pain, on the occasion, we are told, of the departure of his brother to Australia.

Grimly overlooking Parker's Piece, on the site of Queen Anne Terrace, there stood, until demolished about forty years ago, the sombre Borough Gaol. Two of its old cell doors are to be seen on either side of the covered way leading to the main entrance of the New Theatre.

Entering Regent Street from the Piece and turning to our right, we notice across the road Llandaff House (conspicuous on account of its quaint porch) which was, in the latter half of the eighteenth century, the residence of Dr Richard Watson, the non-resident Bishop of Llandaff. This notable personage was not content to be merely a Professor of Divinity, he strayed even further afield in the pursuit of knowledge.

To perfect himself in anatomy he procured on one occasion a body from London, and when he had finished with his subject deposited the dissected remains in a box and commissioned an old soldier to bury it in the fields. The man, however, considering the box too valuable to lose, emptied its contents into the Cam, which was then in flood, and some gruesome fragments of humanity were drifted on shore, with the result that a great hue and cry was aroused for the unknown murderer !

So notorious was the desire of this eminent Divine for further preferment that a local editor, Benjamin Flower, of the *Cambridge Intelligencer*, was prompted to comment upon the matter. For this indiscretion he very soon found himself summoned before the House of Lords for an alleged libel on the Bishop of Llandaff, and was duly sentenced to six months' imprisonment in Newgate and the payment of a fine of £100 !

In later life Dr Watson was attracted by the beauties of Westmoreland, and built for himself a house on the banks of Windermere. In this connection Gunning tells the following story of two rival inn-keepers :

The principal inn at the head of Windermere had been known as the " Cock " ; but the landlord, by way of compliment to his distinguished neighbour, substituted the " Bishop " as the new sign. An inn-keeper close by, who had frequently envied mine host of the " Cock " for his good fortune in securing a considerable preponderance of visitors, took advantage of the

DR RICHARD WATSON, BISHOP OF LLANDAFF.
From an engraving after Romney.

Face page 36

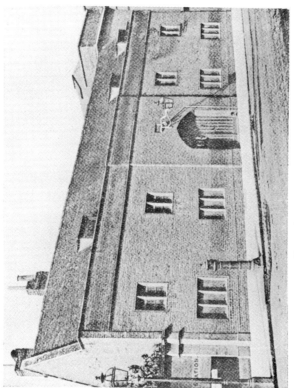

THE SPINNING HOUSE.

Face page 37

change, and attracted many travellers to his house by putting up (himself) the sign of the " Cock." The landlord with the new sign was much discomfited at seeing many of his old customers deposited at his rival's establishment ; so, by way of remedy, he put up in large letters, under the portrait of the Bishop, " THIS IS THE OLD COCK ! "

Continuing our way down the street, the sight of the imposing Borough Police Station recalls the dingy old Spinning House, or Bridewell, founded by Hobson in 1628, which until 1901 stood upon this spot.

This institution, which has figured so largely at times in the social annals of the University and of the Town, was originally intended to provide shelter and employment for those in need, and also " as a house of correction for unruly and stubborn rogues." The Trust of this Charity, which was augmented from time to time by local bequests, and notably by that of John Bowtell, was vested in an equal number of representatives of the University and Town. Under the direction of a resident worsted-weaver, who was appointed Master and Governor, and with provision for "a sufficient stock of wool and flax for setting . . . poor people . . . to work " the industry of spinning was carried out here until the opening years of the nineteenth century.

At this period the University authorities, in order more easily to exercise their ancient powers of summary jurisdiction over the frail daughters of the Town, appear to have arrogated to themselves the premises for the detention and correction of those judged by them to be a public nuisance.

Necessary as these powers may have been in the early days of the University for the protection of their students, they had long been regarded as an anachronism and an annoyance to the town residents. The tide of resentment against this academic " Star Chamber" in their midst increased in volume at each rumour of a "mistaken" arrest till finally in the last decade of the past century, a notorious miscarriage of justice led the University to yield their rights to the civil authorities.[1]

[1] Rights granted to Chancellor's Court by Letters Pat.—Q. Eliz. (1561). Tested and confirmed in 1861 and 1891-2, given up by private Act of Parliament (57 & 58 Vict. c. LX. 9, 5) as result of amicable negotiations between Borough Council and University.

The house (No. 55) over the way, formerly the manse of the Baptist Chapel opposite to it, probably marks the site of the Emmanuel Coffee-house and pleasure grounds opened by John Delaport in 1763, whose lengthy and curiously worded advertisements are fully quoted by Cooper.[1] One of these states that " None but the free, generous, debonnaire, and gay are desired to attend."

The ancient Inn, known as The Castle, a picturesque example of the domestic architecture of the seventeenth century, marks the site of Rudd's Hostel. Records show that, in 1284, Hugh de Balsham, the founder of Peterhouse, presented this hostel to the Hospital of St John, a Religious House once standing upon the site of St John's College.

In the earliest days of the University there were many such hostels scattered about the town, serving as boarding-houses for the students who congregated at Cambridge to attend the lectures at the University Schools ; for better discipline of the students, however, colleges were founded ; and though the hostels were gradually absorbed or suppressed by the colleges, the hostel system flourished as late as the early part of the sixteenth century.

Continuing northwards and turning into Emmanuel Lane, we notice a range of nine quaint tenements known as The Pensionary, an institution built by one Ralph Symonds in, or soon after, the year 1586, for the accommodation, apparently, of the servants of Emmanuel College.[2] The adjoining corner shop occupies the site of a seventeenth century house once known as Roxton Hall.

Regaining St Andrew's Street, our attention is attracted to the recently built premises of No. 21, by the large coat of arms upon its red brick façade. Immediately below these arms may be discerned the sign of The Chalice, commemorating an Inn that once stood on this site.

The useful clock we see on the corner house at the covered entrance to Post Office Terrace, formerly the Brazen George yard, reminds us that this building was once used as the General Post Office. Upon the removal of the Post Office in September 1886, to

[1] *Annals*, IV., pp. 328 and 329.
[2] Dr Stokes, *C. A. S.*, 8vo publications, No. XLVII., 1915, p. 30

its present position, this clock was taken down, but the passers-by were so inconvenienced by its absence that a successful petition was presented to the authorities praying for its replacement.

In St Andrew's Church are two monuments worthy of notice. One of these, on the north wall of the chancel is inscribed to the memory of Captain Cook, the great navigator, and his family ; his widow and two of his sons being buried in the nave of the church. The other, upon the opposite wall, commemorates Thomas Thackeray, a great-uncle of Thackeray the novelist.

In our first Walk we referred to the King's Ditch and the Trumpington Gate, and here, at the juncture of Hobson Street with Sidney Street, was yet another of these mediaeval entrances, known as the Barnwell Gate, where the main road crossed the Ditch on its way to Hobson Street.

Continuing our itinerary, we come to 63 Sidney Street, the Philo Chambers, once the home of the Philo-Union or Cambridge Literary Society, established in 1826. It was first started at the Crown and Woolpack, an Inn which at one time stood on the site now occupied by Lloyds Bank.

Charles Henry Cooper, author of the *Annals of Cambridge*, was one of the Society's most distinguished members, and contributed in no small degree to the success of this Society.

In the early days of the Philo-Union's existence it was customary for the members to regale themselves after the debates with a supper of bread and cheese and ale, which was provided for the modest sum of sixpence ; this, however, on special occasions, such as the marriage of a member, was supplemented by a bowl of punch contributed by the happy man.

In 1846 the Philo-Union found rooms at the Wrestler's Inn, Petty Cury, to the west of the present Post Office, moving to the house in Sidney Street in 1851, where it continued until 1887, when the Society was dissolved. A tablet on the front of the house records that

CHARLES DARWIN
LIVED HERE IN 1828.

He had rooms later in Fitzwilliam Street (see p. 13).

Opposite, on the string-course of the parapet of No. 11, and also on the leaden fall-pipe, may be noticed an emblematic reminder of old Mr Joshua's Lee's pipe-works, namely, two "churchwardens" in saltire.

> Little tube of mighty power,
> Charmer of an idle hour.
> Object of my warm desire :
> Lip of wax, and eye of fire :
> And thy snowy taper waist,
> With my finger gently braced.[1]

High on the spire of Trinity Church may be detected a thermometer ! It was placed there by a parishioner when the spire was re-erected in 1901, in order that he might test the magnifying power of his telescopes by reading the figures on the little instrument.

Closely associated with this church is the name of Charles Simeon, Fellow of King's and Vicar of this parish for 54 years. During the early days of his ministrations this remarkable and earnest evangelist suffered, on account of his calvinistic views, much persecution both from his parishioners and from members of the University, and " for many years," we are told, " Trinity Church and the streets leading to it were the scenes of the most disgraceful tumults."[2]

But when Simeon died in November 1836 an impressive tribute to the singular piety and true worth of the man was made by the vast concourse of people who followed his body to the grave in King's College Chapel, filling the great building to its utmost capacity.

Through the stone entrance gateway, a few paces further on, with its heavily mantled arms of the De la Pryme family, appears the quaintly embattled gabled house (No. 15), the residence successively of Sir Busick Harwood, Professor of Anatomy and, later, of George Pryme, barrister and Professor of Political Economy.

[1] Hone's *Every-Day Book*, 1827. Vol. 2, p. 399.
[2] Gunning's *Reminiscences*, 1854. Vol. 2, p. 147.

Professor Pryme in his *Autobiographic Recollections*, tells us that he purchased this property in 1820, and adds also :

It was a large remnant of the Trinity Hostel, which, with many others of the like kind, were superseded by Colleges. In making considerable alterations I preserved as much as I could the remains of the internal arrangement. At first it seemed as if it would be impossible to remain there, for our servants believed in a rumour that the house was haunted, and for some time we had a difficulty in persuading them to remain, till at length the ghost was laid by ourselves occupying the room in which " the black lady " was said to walk.

The year 1832 saw the Reform Bill passed and Pryme and Spring-Rice returned as Representatives of the Borough. To commemorate the election of the first members upon the extended franchise, their portraits were painted together, on one canvas, which may be seen hanging on the west wall of the large room of the Guildhall.

ENTRANCE GATEWAY TO No. 15, SIDNEY STREET, showing the De la Pryme arms.

Regaining the road we soon come to Sidney Sussex College, where the oriel window looking upon the street, midway between the Gateway and Jesus Lane, is the one usually pointed out to the curious visitor as marking Cromwell's room, although there appears to be little, if any, authority for such an assumption.

Regarding the well-known portrait of the Protector hanging in the College Hall, Walpole tells us that Cromwell, while sitting to Sir Peter Lely, said, " Mr Lely, I desire you would use all your skill to paint my picture truly like me, and not flatter me at all ; but remark all these roughnesses, pimples, warts, and everything as you see me, otherwise I never will pay you a farthing for it."[1]

[1] *Anecdotes of Painting*, 1862, Vol. II., p. 444.

It was on another portrait of Cromwell, painted by Robert Walker, that Elsum wrote his epigram :

> By lines o' th' face and language of the eye,
> We find him thoughtfull, resolute, and sly.[1]

It was at Sidney Sussex, on the evening of 4 March 1869, that a gathering of epicures essayed to prove the reputed virtues of cooked donkey.

By the courtesy of the University Librarian, I have been given access to the late Mr J. W. Clark's notes on the Donkey Dinners, which I now proceed to quote :

Mr A. A. Vansittart, formerly Fellow of Trinity College, was moved to buy a healthy young donkey. He fattened it on oil-cake and at a suitable moment had it killed by a butcher. The idea of eating him was warmly taken up by Hardy of Sidney, whose gastronomic tastes were notorious, and under his direction every part of the animal was utilized. Joints were also given to Trinity and to one or two private friends. I dined on all the occasions . . . and thought the meat delicious, rather like swan. Among the lower orders the proceedings excited the greatest possible disgust, so much so that the man who usually bought the dripping out of Sidney College kitchen refused to take any that week.

On one of the menus appeared an entrée described as " Les Rognons d'Edouard." The following verses are taken from a lengthy street-ballad entitled " The Great Donkey Feed," written to commemorate this singular experiment :

> O have you heard of the dainty feed,
> (It is really true indeed.)
> By some gourmands it was agreed
>   To try a fatted donkey.
>
> All who tasted did thus declare,
> No ven'son, French dish, or hare,
> Could by any means compare,
>   With a roasted donkey.
>
> Knifeum, forkum, feedem fum,
> He haw ! He haw ! He haw hum.
> How do you like your donkey done,
>   The wonderful donkey feeding !

[1] *Ibid.*, p. 422.

MANTELPIECE FROM No. 3, SUSSUM'S YARD,
now at St John's College.

Face page 43

The well-known house in Bridge Street (No. 4) with iron rings under the eaves and grotesque masks above the windows was built, together with the adjoining house, in 1729, and has been known successively as Ye Bell Inn and The Hoop. Though the glories of The Hoop are now past, its fame is immortalised by Wordsworth in his *Prelude* :

> Onward we drove beneath the Castle ; caught,
> While crossing Magdalene Bridge, a glimpse of Cam ;
> And at the Hoop alighted, famous Inn.

Till well past the middle of the last century, the Hoop was the headquarters of the Whig party, the Eagle in Bene't Street being that of the Tories.

The fine old red brick façade on the opposite side of the road dated, on the heads of the two rainpipes, 1791, conceals a much older building which may possibly have been the residence of Lowry, who lies buried in St Sepulchre's churchyard, and, together with Cromwell, represented the Borough in the Long Parliament.

For many years this house was the property and residence of Sir Isaac Pennington, M.D. (1745-1817), an eminent physician of his day, Professor of Chemistry and, later, Regius Professor of Physic in the University, who bequeathed the premises to St John's, of which college he was senior Fellow.

Another notable occupant of this house was Lord Houghton, who lodged here when an undergraduate.

Carved immediately above the mud-splashed west door of the tower of St Clement's Church are the words " Deum Cole," the punning motto of that distinguished county antiquary, the Reverend William Cole, F.S.A. (1714-1782). He was born at Little Abington, and having been educated at Eton, where his principal friend and companion was Horace Walpole, and at Clare and King's Colleges, ended his days at Milton in this county. Cole left his copious MSS. to the British Museum on condition that they should not be opened until twenty years after his death, and the greatest curiosity was aroused as the expiration of this period drew near. They consist of nearly one hundred folio volumes, and form a mine of information for the historian of Cambridgeshire.

Cole's intentions were that the tower and spire should be built over the graves of his two sisters, which lie north of the west end of the church, and appointed Essex, one of his executors, to undertake the work. Essex, however, died soon after Cole, and it was not until nearly forty years later that the steeple was built (1821), and then in wanton disregard of the benefactor's designs. Observe the weather vane representing, Cooper tells us in his *Memorials*, the crest of Charles Humfrey, the architect of this very poor piece of work, but which seems to us to bear a far greater resemblance to the crest of Cole, namely, a demi-dragon holding a javelin in its dexter claw.

The man in the street may similarly be in doubt as to the pointer of the vane. It may merely be the conventional arrow, but we like to think it is intended for a quill-pen expressive of Cole's life-long industry as a writer on antiquities.

The Parish Registers of St Clement's contain many references to outbreaks of the plague in Cambridge, and the following entries show the havoc wrought by the epidemic in a single family in less than a week :

1603. Parishners . . . which died and were buried upon the greene in the plaigue time, viz. . . . .
Eliz. the daughter of Xpofer Jakes buried there the 25 of October 1603.
Chrofer Jakes and another childe of his, buried there 28 of October 1603.
Alice Jakes late wief of Xpofer Jakes buried there 29 of October, 1603.

The " greene " was probably Midsummer Common, then known as Jesus Green, and, in earlier times called Grenecroft. One or more plague pits seem to have been used for burials, and victims appear to have been buried as soon as possible after death.

A second outbreak in 1665 is indicated in the Registers by the ominous words " The Visitation Begane." When time permitted the cause of death is noted in each case as : " Spotted ffeaver " ; " died off the pestilent ffeaver " ; " died off the disease " ; " died off the plague " ; but when the epidemic was at its height a long list of names follows the comprehensive sentence, " Burialls at the Grene and Pestehouse ffor the Parrish ffrom August the 15th, 1665 . . ." So great, however, was the fear inspired by this terrible

W. WEST

Bird's Yard
Cambridge.

YARD OF OLD CROSS KEYS INN.

scourge that the cause of death, when other than the plague, is often mentioned at this period, sometimes in quaint and obscure terms. Thus a woman is stated to have died in 1665 " off the rising off the lightes " (? inflammation of the lungs) ; more than one child is said to have lost his life " in breeding his teeth " ; and an infant is notified as having " died off the Crushes."

Almost facing the church is the entrance to the yard of the old Red Lion Inn, one of the reputed haunts of the celebrated highwayman known as Dick Turpin (1706-1739).

Crossing the Great Bridge we notice on approaching the street frontage of Magdalene, the figure of a chained swan on the apex of the gable facing us. This heraldic device commemorates the more ancient name of this House, viz. Buckingham College, the arms of whose founder, Stafford, Duke of Buckingham, have, as supporters, two swans proper, chained.

Sharing the fate of other monastic houses, Buckingham College was suppressed in 1529, and three years later its site was granted to Lord Audley by Henry VIII. for the foundation of Magdalene College. Fuller, in his usual humorous style, ventures an explanation of the common pronunciation of the name " Maudlin " :

Thomas, Lord Audley of Walden, Chancellour of England by license obtained from King Henry the eighth—changed Buckingham into Magdalen (vulgarly) Maudlin College, because (as some will have it) his sirname is therein contained betwixt the Initial and Final letters thereof: M'audley'n."

We now enter the oldest part of Cambridge, spoken of till quite recently as the Borough, its residents being known as Borough boys. There was, until a few years ago, in Northampton Street (No. 19) a public-house known by the sign of The Borough Boy.

The quaint overhanging house (No. 25) opposite the entrance to Magdalene College (once the Cross Keys Inn), formerly contained fine oak panelling and a richly carved mantelpiece. These have recently been removed and utilised in fitting up a new Combination Room at Magdalene.

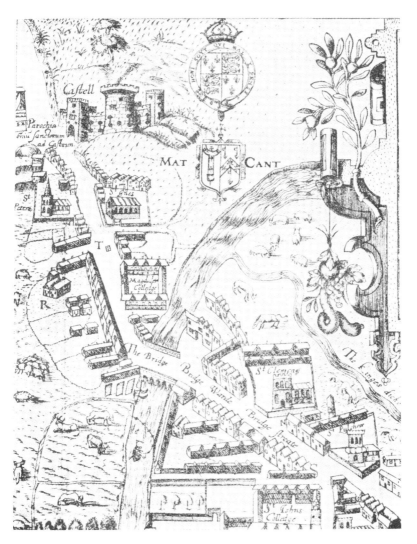

CAMBRIDGE CASTLE, from Lyne's map of 1574.

Oak Mantelpiece from Old Cross Keys Inn, now at Magdalene College.

Face page 47

Advancing a few steps further we come to No. 15, once the residence of Edward Storey (died 1693), formerly an Alderman of Cambridge, and founder of Storey's Charity, whose name is now further perpetuated in Storey's Way.

During the closing years of the eighteenth century, Northampton Street, formerly known as Bell Lane, was the haunt of a notorious burglar named Richard Kidman, who for some years, undetected, had visited several of the College butteries and carried off valuable silver plate. Gunning tells us :

The Colleges were in the greatest state of alarm, each expecting to be plundered that had not before suffered. The most absurd reports were in circulation . . . nor was it until 1801 that the slightest clue was obtained to elucidate these mysterious robberies.

In the early part of that year the house of Mr Alderman Butcher, in St Andrew's Street, was entered by picklock-keys, and a variety of plate stolen. A man named Grimshaw, who had a short time previously swept Mr Butcher's chimneys, was strongly suspected. This man had . . . a small house, on a piece of waste land adjoining the road leading to Newmarket. A strict search was made, but as it proved a fruitless one, Mr Butcher ordered that the house should be pulled down, when a large portion of the stolen plate was discovered. As Grimshaw and Kidman had been so frequently seen together, constables were immediately sent to search his house, where they found a silver pint-pot belonging to Caius College, which Kidman was in the constant habit of using, and twenty-seven teaspoons, from which no pains had been taken to erase the college marks . . . Grimshaw was tried at the following spring assizes, convicted, and subsequently executed, Kidman's sentence was transportation for life.

The sequel to the story runs as follows :

In 1810 great consternation spread through the town on the intelligence being received that Kidman had returned. . . It seems that at the penal settlement he had behaved well, and it is said that on one occasion the clock, by which the convicts worked, was out of order, and no one there could repair it. Kidman proposed to try his hand and succeeded ; this brought him into notice and got him similar work ; he also shewed great skill in gardening, so that when on the occasion of the Jubilee of King George the Third, the Commander was allowed to free some of the convicts, Kidman was amongst those chosen, as one of the best behaved. . . . He came back to Cambridge, where he lived a quiet and respectable life for some years, and used to go about cleaning clocks and doing gardening.

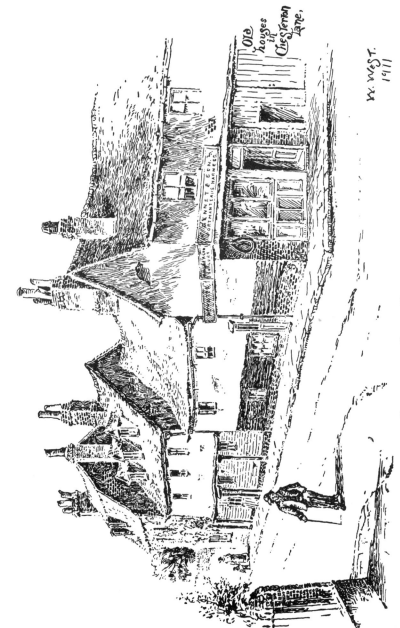

Old houses in Chesterton Lane.

W. WEST.
1911

CHESTERTON LANE CORNER IN 1911.

Leaving Northampton Street and turning up the Castle Hill we pass at the corner the Old White Horse Inn, interesting on account of a hiding hole used, probably, in earlier days, by highwaymen and ingeniously contrived in the exceptionally wide central chimney breast. The little hiding place was entered from a sitting room through an aperture at the back of a fireplace, now walled up.

The clock, seen on the west end of St Giles' Church, has a more interesting history than its plain face would lead one to suppose, for originally it graced the old clock-house that occupied, till 1817, the

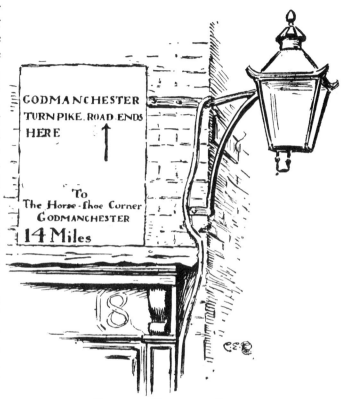

TURNPIKE BOUNDARY STONE.

space between the N.E. turret and the first northern buttress of King's Chapel.[1] It was then removed to the western wall of St Giles', and after the demolition of that building in 1875, and the erection of the existing church, was placed in its present position. The chancel arch of the original early Norman church is still preserved in the south aisle of the new building. This appears to be a fragment of the little Augustinian Canonry built in 1092 by Picot, the Norman sheriff of Cambridgeshire. The House was founded

[1] See Vernon and Hood, *Beauties of England*, 1801.

in fulfilment of a joint vow made by Picot and his wife Hugolina when her life was despaired of, and was afterwards removed to and incorporated in Barnwell Priory.

Opposite St Giles' Church, high up on the house numbered 8, is the boundary-stone of the old turnpike road from Godmanchester ; the toll-house, however, was at the Histon Road junction. Close by stands all that is left of St Peter's Church. Roman bricks (bearing some resemblance to rough red tiles) have been incorporated into its walls and are easy to discover on the south side. Many records of Roman occupation have been found in this neighbourhood, and we illustrate a small Roman bas-relief, six inches long and four wide, said to have been taken from the foundations of St Peter's, and at one time to have been inserted into the wall of a cottage facing the south side of the Church.[1]

BASSO-RELIEVO ON A ROMAN BRICK.

Immediately opposite the Shirehall stands Ye Olde Three Tuns, a picturesque Inn dating back to the sixteenth century. Although not averse to more than one hostelry in the town, it was here, on its outskirts, that Dick Turpin usually stayed when visiting Cambridge, occupying a bedroom, now destroyed, at the back of the house.

The first milestone that we reach on the Huntingdon Road bears the inscription " Cambridge ½ mile," a statement which may seem questionable to the weary pedestrian. The distance, however, is not in this case measured from the point on St Mary's noted during our first Walk, but from the Shirehall, a building which marks the old boundary of the Borough and County.

[1] Storer and Grieg, *Antiquarian and Topographical Cabinet . . . of views . . in Great Britain*, 1807, Vol. II.

Ye Olde Three Tuns.

CHAPTER IV.

Cambridge Revisited

4

HE previous three Walks in Cambridge having taken us respectively south, west, and northwards ; it seems but fitting that we should now complete the cardinal points of the compass by making our next and last expedition eastward in the direction of Barnwell, and with this object in view the Bridge Street corner of Jesus Lane will be found a convenient point of departure.

Before leaving this spot, however, let us first recall a few of its old associations. Across the road, on a site now covered by Whewell's Courts, stood the Dolphin, a Tudor inn long since forgotten, yet of great repute in its day, when it sheltered a martyr and saw the reception of a prince. Here Thomas Cranmer, afterwards Archbishop of Canterbury, having forfeited his fellowship at Jesus College owing to his marriage, resided with his wife Joan, who was a niece of the landlady. After his wife's untimely death, he was re-elected to his fellowship, and, in later years when he had fallen from his high estate, his dead wife was derisively spoken of as Black Joan of the Dolphin.

Our local diarist, Alderman Samuel Newton, in an entry dated 26 November 1670, describes, in the following terms, the reception by the Corporation of the Prince of Orange upon the occasion of his visit to the University :

. . . . The Aldermen in scarlett, and the Common Counsell and other Gownemen in their habitts being ready at the Dolphin Inne, mett and saluted the Prince at the hither end of Jesus Lane against the Dolphin, just upon the Turne of his Coach. . . .

My next note of reference to this important inn is in connection with the finding of treasure-trove, and runs as follows :

. . . As some workmen were digging for the foundations of a building in the cellar of the old Dolphin Inn, below the spot once occupied by the late Alderman Newling's coal yard, about four feet from the surface they struck into a soil of black mould, above which the ground had been artificially raised, probably when the Dolphin was erected. Here they found the mouldered remains of a leather bag, out of which there fell, jingling, a parcel of gold rings, containing precious stones, in very ancient setting ; also some old silver coins, and other articles of value. . . .[1]

A descriptive list of the articles follows, in which the " old silver coins " are specified as " silver pennies of Henry the Third, struck in his fifty-first year . . ." about which time, it is added, " they seem to have been buried."

The date of these coins, 1266, and the situation of the Dolphin in the Old Jewry, point to this long-hidden treasure having been buried, for safety, by a Jew. The Jews, who were suffering much persecution about this period, were expelled from England in 1290, and their houses confiscated to the King.

The site in question has also yielded other objects of antiquarian interest, and a selection of these now deposited in Trinity College Library, has been fully described by the late Mr William White.[2] The most remarkable articles were rescued during certain excavations by the late Mr Alderman Elliot Smith, who presented them to the College ; one is " a beautiful fibula " (or brooch), " studdied with rubies, and of Saxon workmanship " ; another and more valuable find consists of " five gold rings, each set with a precious stone and found upon the right hand of a skeleton, one upon each finger."

Time passed, the old Dolphin was swept away, and there arose in its place a series of houses which may be briefly reviewed. At the southern corner of Dolphin Lane, or All Saints' Passage, as it now began to be called, stood the shop of Bulstrode ; next to this came the large stone-fronted house of Finch (looking down Jesus Lane), still further south stood a smaller house occupied by

[1] *Cambridge Chronicle*, 5 Sept. 1817.   [2] *C. A. S. Proc.*, N.S., Vol. II., 1895, p. 299.

Bell, and beyond, adjoining the old Mews Inn yard, that of Creeke ;
traces of the weather-markings of the latter building can be seen on
the northern wall of No. 35, Sidney Street.   The Cambridge Philosophical Society occupied rooms over Bulstrode's shop from 1820
to 1833, when it moved into its new building (now the Hawks' Club)
overlooking All Saints' Churchyard.   This house eventually proved
to be too expensive, and in 1865 was sold.   The Society's Museum
was presented to the University, when, in the capable hands of the
late Mr J. W. Clark, it helped to form the nucleus of the present fine
Museum of Zoology, and the Society itself with its library moved
to its present quarters at the New Museums, near Pembroke
Street.

In due course, Bulstrode's shop and the adjoining houses which
supplanted the Dolphin Inn were themselves swept away in
order to make room for the present sombre extension to Trinity,
already referred to as Whewell's Courts.   Before leaving, we
may note on its rain-pipes the monogram " W. W." of the great
Master of Trinity, to whose generosity this building is due.   William
Whewell played a large and distinguished part in early Victorian
Cambridge.

> Gaunt, stern, and stalwart, with broad brow set squarely
>   O'er the fierce eye, and the granite-hewn jaw.
>
> . . . . .
>
> Son of a hammer-man : right kin of Thor, he
>   Clove his way through, right onward, amain ;
> Ruled when he'd conquered, was proud of his glory,—
>   Sledge-hammer smiter, in body and brain.

—so Tom Taylor describes this striking personality.   Such a man
was naturally the subject of witticisms and anecdotes.   One of
his best-known contributions to science, a treatise *Of the Plurality
of Worlds*, was said to prove that " through all infinity, there was
nothing so great as the Master of Trinity."   Sydney Smith said of
him, " Science is his forte and Omniscience his foible."   A note in
the pages of *Punch* alluding to his supposed desire for ecclesiastical
preferment and punning upon his name, states that : " The amiable
Master was heard to say, ' Let *who will* be next Bishop, I shall

ELECTION SCENE IN 1830.
Chairing Lord Osborne and Mr Adeane to the Hoop Inn.

Face page 54

be satisfied.' " His splendid physique, too, is said to have inspired an admiring pugilist to exclaim, " What a man was lost when they made you a parson ! " But we must dismiss as apocryphal a good story which has already found its way into print concerning an alleged dispute between Queen Victoria and the Master as to their respective claims to Trinity Lodge. Again, the tale that he was reproved for wearing his cap in the presence of royalty, in assertion of a supposed privilege of the Masters of Trinity, may be dismissed as still more frivolous. Anyone who cares to look into Mr Rouse Ball's interesting *Notes on Trinity College* will find that although many times honoured by the presence of royalty, its Lodge is not a royal residence, and his Majesty's judges are lodged there by the courtesy of the Master and Fellows. It was, indeed, Whewell himself who, by making it a test case in 1863, settled this point, and it is worth recording that the Judges were quartered before 1606 at the Dolphin Inn.

During the contest for the University Chancellorship between the Prince Consort and Lord Powis, resulting in the Prince's success, Whewell threw all his weight on the royal side. The numbers of *Punch* during this period (March, 1847) are full of skits and sketches dealing with the great event, including a representation of the Public Orator, Mr Crick, declaiming to the new Chancellor an Address, of which a metrical version[1] is given, ending as follows :

From faction's sacrilegious claws
  Keep Church and Bishopric ;
Support our academic cause :
Uphold our rights, defend our laws,
  (Ejaculated Crick).

The speech was done. He made a pause
  For Albert and for Vic ;
Three most vociferous huzzaws
Then broke from mighty Whewell's jaws,
Who, as proof of his applause,
Straight to the buttery goes and draws
  A pint of ale for Crick.

[1] From the pen of Thackeray.

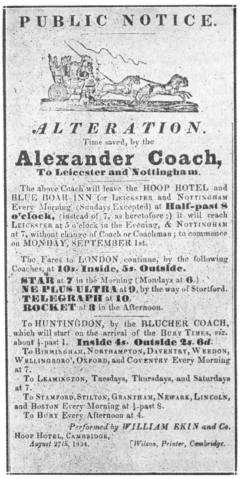

COACHING TIME-TABLE, 1834.

Turning now into Jesus Lane, or Nuns' Lane, as it was formerly called, a few yards bring us to a fine wrought-iron gate, made by a local craftsman named Audley for a more suitable position, but now brushed aside by every hawker and dustman who enters the mean passage (adjoining No. 5) to which it gives access.

We next come to the premises of the Pitt Club, whose classic frontage does not seem so incongruous when we consider that it was built by the Roman Bath Company. The principal promoter of this venture was Henry Staples Foster, Mayor in 1849, but the greater attractions for bathers afforded by the upper river prevented the company from becoming a financial success. This building occupies what was originally the site of the entrance to the once busy inn yard of the Hoop, whence every day rumbled out four coaches to London, and others respectively to Huntingdon, Birmingham, Stamford and Bury, and (on Tuesdays, Thursdays, and Saturdays) to Leamington. This was in 1834, when the fare to London was only 5s., whilst to-day, after a lapse of nearly a century, the journey costs us 8s. 1d.

JESUS LANE IN 1805.

THE FRIENDS' MEETING HOUSE, 1888.

Face page 56

A few steps further bring us to a modern red brick building with an iron gate beneath an arch, whence we may dimly see the Meeting House of the Society of Friends, now only a small body in the town, but having traditions dating back to the days of its founder, George Fox. When excavating for the foundations of this new building and gateway in 1894, a number of human skeletons were unearthed in which a late learned anatomist was much interested. The story goes that at a meeting of the Cambridge Antiquarian Society he said the type of the skulls was not Roman, British, or Saxon, and must be referred to a prehistoric tribe. Our professor was much discountenanced when somebody rose and asked if he was aware that the site was that of a Quaker burial ground! In his *Journal*, Fox records the rough reception he got from the scholars, when on a visit to Cambridge in 1655 ; the Mayor, however, gave him safe asylum at his house, where, as Fox tells us, " We sent for the Friendly People, and had a fine meeting there in the power of God." Four years later (1659) we find the University Librarian publicly disputing with Fox and his colleagues at their Meeting House, " opposite Sidney College Gate," against the tenets of Quakerism. Whether this meeting-place really stood in Sidney Street, opposite to the College Gate or not, at least the chief memories of the " Friendly People " linger in Jesus Lane—indeed as early as 1698-9 meetings were held there at the house of a shoemaker named Brazier. For frequenting these Quaker gatherings, the Register of Jesus College records the expulsion, at that time, of Roger Kelsall, one of the students. It is more than likely that the existing building occupies the very site on which Brazier's house stood.

The old Meeting House has had a varied and useful existence, and served at one time for the Jesus Lane Sunday School, founded in 1827, which has survived to carry on its valuable work to this day. Queens' men played a prominent part in the foundation of this school, but whether the scheme was originated by one or by several is a matter upon which history is somewhat obscure. One account attributes the idea to William Leeke, then an undergraduate of Queens' College (father of a well-remembered Vicar of St Andrew-the-Less), whilst another divides the credit between Messrs. Wright,

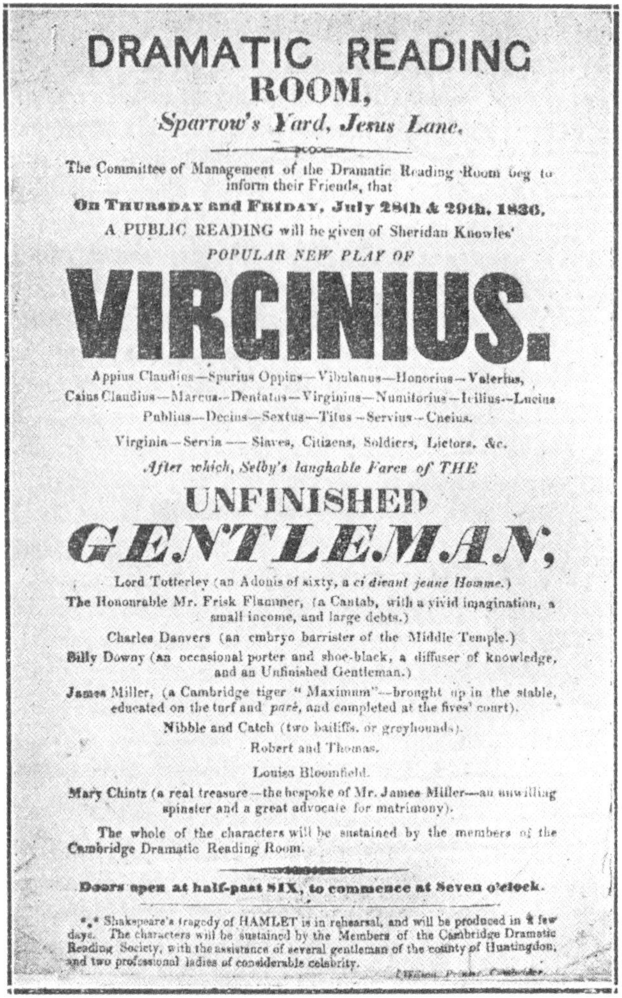

DRAMATIC READING ROOM,

Sparrow's Yard, Jesus Lane.

The Committee of Management of the Dramatic Reading Room beg to inform their Friends, that

On Thursday and Friday, July 28th & 29th, 1836,

A PUBLIC READING will be given of Sheridan Knowles'

POPULAR NEW PLAY OF

VIRGINIUS.

Appius Claudius—Spurius Oppius—Vibulanus—Honorius—Valerius, Caius Claudius—Marcus—Dentatus—Virginius—Numitorius—Icilius—Lucius Publius—Decius—Sextus—Titus—Servius—Cneius.

Virginia—Servia —— Slaves, Citizens, Soldiers, Lictors, &c.

After which, Selby's laughable Farce of THE

UNFINISHED *GENTLEMAN*,

Lord Totterley (an Adonis of sixty, a *ci devant jeune Homme.*)

The Honourable Mr. Frisk Flammer, (a Cantab, with a vivid imagination, a small income, and large debts.)

Charles Danvers (an embryo barrister of the Middle Temple.)

Billy Downy (an occasional porter and shoe-black, a diffuser of knowledge, and an Unfinished Gentleman.)

James Miller, (a Cambridge tiger "Maximum"—brought up in the stable, educated on the turf and *pavé*, and completed at the fives' court).

Nibble and Catch (two bailiffs, or greyhounds).

Robert and Thomas.

Louisa Bloomfield.

Mary Chintz (a real treasure—the bespoke of Mr. James Miller—an unwilling spinster and a great advocate for matrimony).

The whole of the characters will be sustained by the members of the Cambridge Dramatic Reading Room.

Doors open at half-past SIX, to commence at Seven o'clock.

*** Shakspeare's tragedy of HAMLET is in rehearsal, and will be produced in a few days. The characters will be sustained by the Members of the Cambridge Dramatic Reading Society, with the assistance of several gentleman of the county of Huntingdon, and two professional ladies of considerable celebrity.

JESUS LANE THEATRE PLAYBILL, 1836.

Hiscock, Marsh, and Clarke, of Queens', and Harden of St John's. However this may be, these men, with a few friends, formed an earnest little band of workers who canvassed Barnwell for scholars, and were rewarded for their zeal by an attendance of about 220 on the opening Sunday. Some six years later, the school, having outgrown the Meeting House, migrated to King Street. Here success followed upon success, and when still further room was necessary, the present schools in Paradise Street were built, and subsequently opened on 31 October, 1867.

In 1855, the Meeting House was let to the Corporation for the purpose of accommodating the newly-formed Borough Free Library, but the latter soon became too important to be quartered (as stated at the time) " in the cool shade, in an out-of-the-way lane, and up a dark passage," and, accordingly, in June, 1862, it was moved to its present more fitting premises at the Guildhall.

Looking into Park Street, we can see, adjoining the Meeting House, an ugly mass of brickwork, rising above a forsaken shop, once the Hoop tap-room. This building was erected by the Union Society, and occupied by them from 1831 until 1850, when they abandoned it for the " dingy old room in Green Street," formerly a Dissenting Chapel. After the exit of the Union Society these Park Street premises were used as billiard rooms until taken over by the A.D.C. in 1860, and converted into the compact little theatre and auditorium existing to-day.

The connection of Jesus Lane with amateur dramatic art has been long and interesting. Though academic plays and masques, for centuries, had been staged in our College halls and inn-yards, interest in the regular drama was traditionally discountenanced by the University authorities. In the opening years of the last century, however, a real and lively enthusiasm for the stage began to manifest itself in the formation of sundry dramatic societies, and the Shakespeare Club appears to be the earliest of which any records can now be traced. This club was formed in 1830, but had a chequered existence, and gave place in 1833 to the excellent Garrick Club, whose list of members included such names as Henry Rance, William

U.A.P. PLAYBILL, 1835

Haddon Smith, and Harry Hall, the last gratefully remembered for his splendid gift of Shakespearian literature to the Free Library.

In addition to the Garrick, which seems to have attracted the most capable players, there flourished another Society, calling itself the Cambridge Dramatic Reading Room, and I have before me a play-bill announcing performances by its members for 28 and 29 July 1836, at Sparrow's Yard, Jesus Lane. These three clubs were formed by the townsfolk, but in 1835 another venture known as the " U.A.P." had been started, as appears from an advertised performance of " The Rivals " for 23 March in that year, followed by the farce " High Life Below Stairs." Whether these cryptic letters, " U.A.P." signify " University Amateur Players " I do not know, but on the playbill in my possession a contemporary hand has added the names of the actors, who were members of the University. With regard to Sparrow's Yard, we learn from another source of information that here a body of undergraduates provided funds for a certain Andrew J. Tempany to build and run the Jesus Lane Theatre, and upon its boards members of all these Societies, University and other, would seem to have appeared at various times. This evidently was no mean building. We are told that it contained two tiers of boxes, and a good pit ; its stage was said to be forty feet in depth with a proscenium slightly wider than that of the Barnwell Theatre.

Of the many Dramatic Clubs that have been launched, at one time or another, in Cambridge, by townspeople or undergraduates, none has achieved the permanent success of the Amateur Dramatic Club, commonly known as the " A.D.C.," founded in 1855, by Sir Francis Burnand (formerly editor of *Punch*), when an undergraduate at Trinity. The history of the " A.D.C. " is the history of the emancipation of the drama in Cambridge from the arbitrary control of the University authorities. Prominently associated with the club was that great enthusiast on all matters touching the stage, the late Mr John Willis Clark who, when the University in 1870 contemplated its suppression, saved the club from an involuntary dissolution by his tactful influence with the authorities.

The difficulties that beset the early days of the club were many, and Burnand, in his racy *Reminiscences*, speaks as follows of the precautions deemed necessary to be taken by himself and his friends :

To ensure our safety by flight in case of a raid of Proctors, we had a speaking-tube run through from the Hoop bar to our green-room, by which " the office could be given " in an emergency, and outside the windows of the stage we had a ladder placed, by which the performers could have descended into a yard below, and so out to the street, dressed in our (*sic*.) caps and gowns, which would hide the theatrical costume underneath.

However, in 1861, King Edward VII., then Prince of Wales, was elected an honorary member of the club, and doubtless it was to his good-natured encouragement and acceptance of the Honorary Presidency that the " A.D.C." owed its first recognition by the University.

We may well conclude our remarks upon the club with the following apposite lines written by the late Sir Richard Jebb:

O for the skill to trace from page to page,
Through years gone by, the annals of our stage :
To hail those sprightly authors of our choice
In whom the lighter Muse has found a voice.
Burnand, Tom Taylor, ever seen with zest.
Pinero, Henry Byron, and the rest.

.   .   .   .   .   .

O may one loyal aim, through times to be,
Still knit the brethren of the A.D.C.[1]

Until comparatively recent times, Park Street was known as Garlic Fair Lane, for here, as late as 1808, was held the fair granted to the nuns of St Radegund in 1438. The remarkable name of this fair has never been satisfactorily explained. It was also called the Nuns' Fair, and originally was held in the Nuns' Close, the site of the fair-yard being approximately opposite to Manor Street.

The present narrow way of this unlovely street marks the course of the King's Ditch, an interesting water-course made, or rather re-made, at the instance of Henry III. It began its course at the end of Mill Lane at the Mill pool, took approximately the line of Pembroke Street, curved round through St Tibbs' Row and Hobson's Street to Sidney College gardens, passing on its way to the

---

[1] From *Epilogue* spoken at the A.D.C. on 25 Feb. 1905.

lower river through a still existing but buried stone bridge beneath
Jesus Lane opposite Park Street, and so forming a large part of the
boundary of the mediaeval town. A considerable section of the
ditch in this locality was still open, it is said, in 1818.

Little Trinity.
Jesus Lane.

Resuming our way down Jesus Lane, we soon reach a fine
Queen Anne red brick house, set back from the road in its own
grounds, its characteristic pediment and array of carved urns half
buried beneath a veil of Virginia creeper.

This picturesque house is Little Trinity. The site in Queen Elizabeth's time was known as Kimbold's tenement, but the house has little history, and even the origin of its singular name is unknown. Here in mid-Victorian times, lived that well-known "coach," Charlie Crosse, whose charming and hospitable wife lavishly entertained her husband's pupils, made Little Trinity tea parties famous, and held quite a salon for the undergraduates of the time. Crosse was a typical sporting parson, who rode to hounds and patronised all other available sports with inextinguishable zest and spirit. I well remember how this worthy man for very many years spared from his trophies of the chase a fine hare for my father, with the invariable assurance that it was a coursed hare. Hares which fall to the courser are said to be more tender than those which fall to the gun, and my youthful recollections of the family's application to the excellencies of this annual gift give me no cause to doubt the veracity of its generous donor.

Our next object of interest is the ivy-mantled Georgian stone gateway standing at the far end of the ancient wall built by the Franciscans who, in early times, occupied the enclosed Sidney College grounds. This originally stood in Sidney Street, opening into the Court facing the Master's Lodge, and there served as the main entrance to the College. In 1832 the present imitation of a mediaeval gateway-tower was made, and the old gateway relegated to its present position.

Malcolm Street takes its name from a benefactor to the nunnery of St Radegund, no less a personage than Malcolm IV., King of Scotland. Opposite are the derelict stable premises of Messrs. Death and Dyson, well known by an earlier generation as Sparrow's Yard, where once stood the Jesus Lane Theatre already referred to.

All lovers of Cambridge will look with respect upon the large red brick house (No. 32) adjoining the Fellows' garden of Jesus College, which was for many years the residence of Charles Henry Cooper, F.S.A., whose monumental works upon the history and antiquities of his adopted town form a priceless mine of information upon the subjects with which they deal, and, in the words of the late

Entrance Gateway,
Jesus College.

Professor J. E. B. Mayor, " two hundred years hence . . . will be more cited than any other Cambridge books of our time." Cooper, who came of an old Berkshire family, was appointed Town Clerk of Cambridge in 1849, and died in 1866, without having received any honour from the University.

Opposite stands the Clergy School, known as Westcott House, built in 1899 ; and here, though appreciably in front of the present building-line, stood that range of quaint old cottages familiarly known to us as the " Barracks," and by an earlier generation, as " Pigs' Barracks," owing to their being occupied principally by Johnians. Many explanations of the singular and undeserved title " Johnian Hogs " have been given, but none is entirely satisfactory, and the subject is too lengthy to be discussed here. That the expression was well known as early as the year 1679 appears from an entry made in that year by Abraham de la Pryme, of St John's, in his diary. When the austere Dr Gower left the lodge of Jesus College where he had been more feared than loved, in order to assume the mastership of St John's, our diarist writes :

Our master, they say, is [a] mighty high proud man. . . . He came from Jesus College to be made master here, and he was so sevear that he was commonly called the divel of Jesus ; and when he was made master here some unlucky scholars broke this jest upon him,—that now the divel was entered into the heard of swine ; for us Jonians are called abusively hoggs.[1]

Our arrival at the gate of Jesus College recalls the well-known saying of James I. that " were he to choose, he would pray at King's, dine at Trinity, and study and sleep at Jesus," and to this day the beautiful buildings of Bishop Alcock's Foundation remain secluded amidst peaceful surroundings eminently suited to repose.

Towering high above the wall of the Fellows' garden may be noticed the magnificent Oriental Plane, raised by Edward Daniel Clarke in 1802 from seed brought by him from Thermopylae. Clarke, the first Professor of Mineralogy, was known as " Stone " Clarke, to distinguish him from " Bone " Clark, the Professor of Anatomy, and " Tone " Clarke, otherwise John Clarke Whitfield, Professor of Music.

---

[1] *Diary of Abraham de la Pryme, Surtees Soc. Publ.* No. 54, 1870, p. 20.

St Radegund's Manor House, from an old water-colour sketch.

Face page 67

Mr Arthur Gray, Master of Jesus, in his interesting History of the College, gives us the following lively anecdote of " Stone " Clarke as an undergraduate and of the balloon made by him in his third year :

This balloon, which was magnificent in its size and splendid in its decorations, was constructed and manœuvred, from first to last, entirely by himself. It was the contrivance of many anxious thoughts and the labour of many weeks, to bring it to what he wished ; and when at last it was completed to his satisfaction, and had been suspended for some days in the College Hall, of which it occupied the whole height, he announced a time for its ascent. There was nothing at that period very new in balloons or very curious in the species which he had adopted ; but by some means he had contrived to disseminate not only within the walls of his own College, but throughout the whole University a prodigious curiosity respecting the fate of his experiment On the day appointed a vast concourse of people was assembled, both within and around the College ; and the balloon, having been brought to its station, the grass-plot within the cloisters, was happily launched by himself, amidst the applause of all ranks and degrees of gownsmen, who had crowded the roof as well as the area of the cloisters, and filled the contiguous apartments of the Master's Lodge. The whole scene, in short, succeeded to his utmost wish ; nor is it easy to forget the delight which flashed from his eyes and the triumphant wave of his cap when the machine, with its little freight (a kitten), having cleared the College battlements, was seen soaring in full security over the towers of the great gate. Its course was followed on horseback by several persons, who had voluntarily undertaken to recover it ; and all went home delighted with an exhibition upon which nobody but himself would have ventured in such a place.

Turning into Manor Street, the sundry fragments of fluted and other worked stone embodied in the rubble wall on our left, remind us that it is built largely of materials obtained during the extensive restoration of Jesus College Chapel, carried out about 1845. Manor Street forms the eastern boundary of the old Manor garden, whilst All Saints' Vicarage stands, more or less, upon the site of the original Manor House. The latter was demolished about the year 1831, and there is a tradition that it was occupied by John Baskerville, the famous University printer (1758-1765), during his brief residence in Cambridge. Baker's map of Cambridge (1830) clearly indicates the manor buildings and grounds. From recorded recollections of an ancient bedmaker of Jesus College, long since at rest, we learn that in her youth (*c.* 1820) the Manor garden was a neglected wilderness and, near the end of the grounds where Manor Street has since been built, there was a beautiful fountain. This fountain was doubtless supplied by the spring which gave so much trouble to the contractors of the new drainage system in 1895.

Leaving Manor Street we see across the road a small wall-gate, interesting since it occupies the site of the entrance to the Nuns' Close, already alluded to in our reference to Garlic Fair.

The corner House of Belmont Place (No. 62, Jesus Lane) was the residence of John Pratt (1772-1855). Pratt, who was a native of Cambridge and a pupil of Dr Randall (who, as a boy, had sung in Handel's choir), had some local reputation as a composer of Church music, and adapted several anthems from the Masses of Mozart and Haydn, the most popular of these being his version of " Plead Thou my cause." In 1799 he not only succeeded Randall at King's College, but also was appointed University Organist, and that the latter office was no sinecure will be gathered from the following passage taken from the reminiscences of one who knew him well :

The college chapels which maintained a choral service . . . were . . . only three, namely, those of King's, Trinity and St John's Colleges, though Peterhouse indulged its men with a little music of a humble kind on Sunday evenings. At all the other colleges the daily prayers (which the men were compelled to attend) were dreary in the extreme, being simply read in parson-and-clerk fashion. Although there were three chapels with choral foundations, the provision made for the maintenance of the musical services was most meagre and insufficient. There was really but one choir of lay-clerks, and those only six in number, and some of them elderly ; they hastened from chapel to chapel, taking part, on Sundays, in no fewer than six repetitions of the Morning and Evening Service. A single organist had shared with them this almost incredible drudgery ; but in 1842 King's College had engaged a player of its own as deputy for Mr John Pratt, who had grown old and infirm in their service.[1]

On the occasion of the visit of Queen Victoria and the Prince Consort to King's College Chapel in the autumn of 1843, Pratt, though then far advanced in years, played the organ for the last time, when, as the same writer records, he " thundered out Handel's

[1] W. E. Dickson, *Fifty Years of Church Music*, Ely, 1894.

SEAL OF ST RADEGUND'S NUNNERY.

THE GARRICK INN formerly facing the Four Lamps.

Face page 68

' Zadok the Priest ' as the young Queen passed along to the West door, the Provost and Senior Fellows walking backwards before her, and occasionally stumbling as they trod upon their gowns." Commenting upon his personal appearance and temperament, we are told that the aged organist " was a link with the past, keeping up the style of dress and manners in vogue when George the Third was King, and caring little for modern fashions in music or anything else around him."

We cannot pass by the open space at the cross roads, known as the " Four Lamps," without recalling a certain November morning in 1875, when it was the scene of a riotous attack by undergraduates on the Mayor's residence, Poplar House, then standing on the site of the present New Wesleyan Chapel and School. As chief magistrate, John Death had made determined attempts to curb the rowdiness of these young men. Their disorderly conduct had long been a source of much annoyance, and culminated in the breaking up of a concert in the Corn Exchange, at which the Mayor and Corporation were present. Seven arrests were made, and on the following evening the friends of the culprits burnt the effigy of the Mayor on the Market Hill and noisily paraded the streets in the usual " rag " fashion. The morning of the third day of this historic feud saw the Hill thronged with excited undergraduates awaiting the result of the Police Court proceedings, and as soon as their friends heard of the heavy fines inflicted on the seven defendants a mad cry of " To Death's house " was raised. A wild rush to the " Four Lamps " followed; but although the police were able to cope with the furious attack upon the Mayor's house the crowd was not dispersed until considerable damage had been done in the neighbourhood.

The present appearance of Midsummer Common, now laid out in conventional public-park fashion, presents a striking contrast to the once free and open greensward with its meandering ditches and extensive and picturesque level tracts. True, the gargantuan legend, R. Callaby, Dog Fancier, can still be read upon the lime-washed wall, as in the days when Calverley's sporting undergraduate :

> Dropped, at Callaby's, the terrier
> Down upon the prisoned rat,

and true, again, the river still pursues its peaceful course ; but even with these landmarks, it is difficult for members of the present generation clearly to visualise the aspect of the Common before its rich pasture was seared and scarred by modern concrete paths, notice-boards, railings and the roadway leading to the useful, but far from beautiful, iron bridge.

Butt's Green is that portion of the Common which skirts the road from Jesus Lane to Brunswick Walk, its depth extending to the line marked by the dwarf iron boundary-post situated between the Avenue Road and Jesus Close. Here, in ancient times, when archery was an important branch of military service, our ancestors used to practise the art of shooting with the bow. Cooper, in his *Annals*, tells us that in 1351 :

> The County of Cambridge was required to raise 100 archers for the King's passage to France. Of this number, the town was to furnish twenty.

In 1469, the use of the bow by undergraduates in their frequent brawls with the townsfolk was so often attended by serious consequences that the University authorities were compelled to forbid scholars or their servants to carry a bow and arrows without a permit; such permit or licence being given only for " Peaceable purpose and in defence of the University privileges."

Midsummer Fair, or " Pot Fair," as it was familiarly called, owing to the large amount of crockery sold there, was granted by Henry III. to the Priory of Barnwell in 1229, but was subsequently awarded to the town in 1505-6. The Fair has helped to add a new word to our language, for here, during the 16th and the early part of the 17th century, when they were much worn by women, could be bought the gay and tinselled " Tawdrey Laces." St Audrey (or Etheldreda), we are told, was wont, in her youth, to adorn herself with manifold splendid necklaces, and considered the affection of her throat which caused her death to be a punishment for her early vanity. This story gave rise to the quaint custom of selling at her annual fair at Ely silken laces or neckties, known as St Audrey's Laces. The custom spread to other fairs, the name was corrupted to Tawdrey Laces, the emblems of the Saint gradually

POT FAIR. CAMBRIDGE.

Publish'd 25 June 1777

From an engraving by J. Bretherton after Bunbury, 1777.

Face page 70

degenerated into pretentious and gawdy adornments, and the term " Tawdrey " came into common use as a synonym for cheap finery.

In the closing years of the 18th century the fair, which coincided with the gay period of the University Commencement, became a fashionable resort of the local gentry and the members of the University whose hilarious behaviour has been caricatured by the scathing pencil of Bunbury, whilst Gunning, in his *Reminiscences*, completes the details of the picture in the following passage :

The fair on Midsummer Green, known by the name of " Pot Fair," was in all its glory. There were booths at which raffles for pictures, china, and millinery took place every evening, which were not over until a late hour. The Saturday evening preceding the Commencement brought together the greatest assemblage of company ; the gentry in the town and neighbourhood, and many persons from the adjoining counties, used to be present. It was not unfrequently the case that twenty private carriages were in waiting. The promenade extended from the place where the fair is now held to the grounds of Barnwell Abbey. Amongst the company, groups of Masters of Arts, consisting of four or five in a party, who had evidently dined, were to be seen linked arm-in-arm, and compelled all they met with to turn out of the way. Difficult of belief as it may be in the present time, amongst these you might discover many Fellows of Colleges, and not a few clergymen.

On the red brick wall skirting the western end of Butt's Green, can still be seen (1920) sundry white numerals ; and, on each of the buttresses signs of iron staples, formed of old horse-shoes, having been torn away. Here, during that fateful winter of 1914-15, were the horse-lines of a regiment of the gallant 68th Welsh Division, who were billeted, it will be remembered, in the immediate neighbourhood pending orders for overseas. The dates and initials, many entwined with Cupid's symbol, crudely scratched on this battered wall, inspire the hope that this impromptu war shrine may long claim respect from the passer-by.

Following the line of the boundary-fence, to within a few feet of the meadow corner, we may see, on looking through the railings, a lonely grave beneath a chestnut tree, with a headstone inscribed : " Sam, Newfoundland Dog, 1912-18, a Perfect Friend." An officer, whose name is unknown to us, is said to have erected this tribute of affection, creditable alike to poor Sam and his master.

Continuing our walk in the direction of the brick wall that skirts the Common from the Fort St George to Callaby's corner, we find about midway, an ancient door giving access to a garden. This now much battered example of early eighteenth century craftsmanship came from the University Library, where, until about 1887, it opened from what is now known as the History Room into the Schools Quadrangle.

Regaining our main route, the beginning of the great highway to Newmarket, we notice immediately on our right as we ascend the short hill a railed-off and paved footway standing high and dry above the road, and known as Maids' Causeway. This is part of the " sufficient Causey from the further end of Jesus Lane to the hither end of Barnwell " made in accordance with the terms of the will of that great local benefactor, Dr Perse, soon after his death in 1615. In order to understand the meaning of the curious name attached to this section of the " Causey " we must retrace our steps a few hundred yards to the four houses numbered 64-67 in Jesus Lane, facing the Common. On this site once stood the little row of Knight and Mortlock's Almshouses, and in the vestry of All Saints' Church hangs a small framed view of these cottages, with a note stating that they were rebuilt in 1818 by Mr W. Mortlock. (In 1880, the old cottages having become very dilapidated, the trustees built the present more convenient houses in King Street, facing the Wesleyan School.) These almshouses were founded by Elizabeth Knight, of Denny Abbey, spinster, in 1647, for the accommodation of two poor widows and four " poor godly, ancient maidens." In the lease of the ground from the Corporation the site is referred to as " all that piece of waste ground lying in a triangle at a place called Jesus Lane End . . . between the highway leading from Jesus Lane towards Barnwell, . . . Walls' Lane . . . and the then lately erected breastwork." This " breastwork " or " banking-up " is shown in Custance's plan made in 1798, and was no other than Dr Perse's raised causeway. The four old maids, living on an old maid's bounty, would find in Dr Perse's raised path a safe and dry promenade, and there is little doubt that Maids' Causeway derives its strange name from this source.

CAMBRIDGE
GAS-LIGHT AND COKE COMPANY.

Scale of charges per annum for Gas-Light.

SIX DAYS A WEEK FROM DUSK TILL THE HOURS BELOW MENTIONED,

The payments to be made quarterly and as follow:

	NINE O'CLOCK.	TEN O'CLOCK.	ELEVEN O'CLOCK.
	£. s. d. £. s. d.	£. s. d. £. s. d.	£. s. d. £. s. d.
Small Argand Burner. 2. Winter Qrs. each	1 7 0—2 14 0	2. Winter Qrs. each 1 11 6—3 3 0	2. Winter Qrs. each 1 16 0—3 12 0
2. Summer ditto	0 3 0—0 6 0	2. Summer ditto .. 0 2 9—0 5 6	2. Summer ditto ..0 . 2 9—0 5 6
Total per annum	3 0 0	Total per annum 3 8 6	Total per annum 3 17 6
Large Argand Burner. 2. Winter Qrs. each	1 16 0—3 12 0	2. Winter Qrs each 2 0 0—4 4 0	2. Winter Qrs. each 2 7 6—4 15 0
2. Summer ditto	0 3 6—0 7 0	2. Summer ditto .. 0 4 0—0 8 0	2. Summer ditto .. 0 4 6—0 9 0
Total per annum	3 19 0	Total per annum 4 12 0	Total per annum 5 4 0

⁎ One Sixth extra to be charged for all Lights used on Sundays.

Colleges, Private Houses, Inns, and for all Situations in which the Gas is burned to irregular periods,
to be charged as until Eleven o'Clock, or by a special agreement.

Ten Feet of surface pipe will be laid at the Contractors expence; all extra length will be charged Eighteen-pence per foot.—An experienced Fitter has been appointed to furnish all interior Fittings, of whom it is required to execute the work at the lowest charge.

[TURN OVER.

1. OBVERSE.

REGULATIONS.

1. In no case can the Gas be supplied without a glass over each Argand, and none but the straight chimney glass should be used. The flame of the Burner must not exceed three inches in height, as when this is not attended to, the brilliancy of the light is diminished.

2. The lights to be extinguished within quarter of an hour after the expiration of the time for which they were taken, except on Saturday nights, when the burning may continue one hour extra, without additional charge.

3. Should the appertures of the Burners be wilfully widened, the supply of Gas will be discontinued till replaced by new ones, to be paid for by the parties offending; but if any one is detected a second time in this practice, the Contractor must, in justice to himself, discontinue supplying them with Gas altogether.

4. On a refusal to pay the rent one Month after it becomes due, the supply of Gas will be stopped, of which three days notice will be given.

JOHN GRAFTON,
Contractor,

Orders or enquires sent to the new Gas Works, Barnwell, or left with MR. RICHARD NEWBY, Bookseller, Trinity-Street, will receive immediate attention.

Copy of a Certificate from several Gentlemen who have lighted their Private Houses with Gas, at Stamford; in nearly all of those instances the lights have been adopted in the private apartments, generally, and in several of them it is extended to the Bed-Rooms:—

Stamford, March 9th, 1826.

"We, the undersigned, have introduced into our Houses, Offices, and other premises, as might be, the Coal Gas as Manufactured by MR. GRAFTON, at the public works of this place; and can conscientiously declare that it is very pure, sweet and brilliant; that it is utterly divested of smoke or unpleasant smell, or effluvia; and has proved, after twelve months use, in the Drawing-Rooms and best apartments, to be not in the least degree injurious to furniture; moreover, that if used with due care and economy, the consumption of it is by no means extravagant"

WM. BAILEY	ROBERT NICHOLLS SAMUEL JUDD
J. TORKINGTON	ROBERT HUNT J. RODEN
RICHARD TURNHILL	

W. Metcalfe, Printer, Trinity-Street, Cambridge.

2. REVERSE.

In 1680 Alderman Newton writes in his diary, upon the occasion of the visit of Mary of Modena, then Duchess of York, to Cambridge, that the Corporation received her at a house called " New England." All trace of this building has disappeared, but the late Mr John Foster considered that some portion of Maids' Causeway adjoined the site where it stood.

Grafton House takes its name from a former owner and resident, John Grafton, who figures prominently in the annals of street lighting in Cambridge. It was not until 1823 that we find the town lit by gas, and then only by what was known as " oil gas," but a few years afterwards Grafton contracted with the Commissioners for the lighting of our streets with the new " inflammable air or gas obtained from coal." Opening out of Staffordshire Street is Gas Lane, and doubtless it was somewhere in this locality that Grafton first set up his gas-retorts, subsequently removing his plant to the site of the present Company's works, shown in Baker's map of the town in 1830.

In 1834 a company was promoted to take over Grafton's plant and contracts as a going concern, and with this object in view the necessary Parliamentary powers were obtained by an Act passed in the same year.

A few steps bring us to the group of old cottages at the end of Maids' Causeway, next to James Street. Of these the quaintest is the wooden cottage (No. 74) standing shyly back with its little triangular garden between doorway and footpath ; it contains but three rooms, is built of wood throughout, and has weathered the storms of at least a hundred years. In the early part of the 19th century it was the home of one Solomon, the organ blower and bell-ringer of King's Chapel, and from what can be gleaned from the few who dimly remember him, he was no less singular than the little house which sheltered him for so many years.

The first sight of Christ Church gives the impression of an attempted copy of King's Chapel made with model building bricks taken from a child's toybox, just as certain bride-cakes recall the Albert Memorial. The peculiarities of this remarkable specimen of church architecture are not confined to its appearance. It stands due north and south and has no proper chancel, whilst the porch, which it was subsequently found necessary to erect in order to screen off the bitter north winds, is situated in another parish !

Opposite stands Burleigh House, deriving its name from a former owner of the site who held extensive property in the neighbourhood. James Burleigh flourished during the reign of George III., and was one of that small number of public-spirited men who from time to time have risen to affluence by their industry and sterling worth, and played no inconsiderable part in the life of their native town. He followed the remunerative calling of a carrier and, during the stirring times of the Napoleonic menace, was accorded public thanks for his patriotic offer of sixty horses and eight waggons for general service in the event of an invasion. He took also an active part in the volunteer movement of the period. Another sphere of his activities is revealed by the fact that he became a fellow of the Society of Antiquaries. His fine presence, arrayed in the picturesque uniform of a lieutenant of the Cambridge Volunteers of 1798 is well depicted in a full length portrait hanging, together with his sword, in the Free Library, and it is worth noting that among the network of mean streets now covering the once fair fields of Barnwell, James Street and Burleigh Street perpetuate respectively the christian name and surname of this worthy citizen.

The sight of the old theatre building, now a mission hall, awakens interest in the social amenities of a bygone generation whose opportunities for witnessing dramatic performances were confined to the vacations, owing to the rigorous University regulations then prohibiting such forms of entertainment in term-time.

During its life of sixty-three years Barnwell Theatre was visited in succession by most of the great actors of the day, notably Sheridan Knowles, Macready, and Charles Kean, their respective companies being generally supported by the amateur talent provided by the Garrick Club. In 1833 Sheridan Knowles appeared as the hero in his own popular tragedy of " Virginius," and three years later Macready was also seen here in the title rôle of the same play. To the great delight of the play-going public Macready's extended stay enabled him to include Macbeth and Othello in his repertoire.

A short visit of Charles Kean and his wife in 1860 gave Cambridge an opportunity of seeing Kean in his masterly portrayal of the crafty king, Louis XI.

It is interesting to note that in these early days the curtain was raised at 6.30 p.m. and programmes were unknown. Lillo's highly coloured and popular tragedy of " George Barnwell " was usually staged for Horse Fair night, and always drew a crowded pit, where free fights were frequent. On such occasions the timid and frightened sought refuge in the boxes, then well within reach of the pit benches, and, when the rough-and-tumble was over, the play proceeded, and all was soon forgotten by everyone in their tense interest in the machinations of the callous adventuress and the fate of her victim.

The drama in question is founded upon the old ballad of " George Barnwell," whose hero, it may be mentioned, had no connection with the Cambridge suburb.

> A London 'Prentice ruin'd is our theme

states the prologue to the play, piously adding that such a moral tale designed

> . . . thoughtless youth to warn, and shame the age
> From vice destructive, well becomes the stage !

Built in 1814, the Theatre Royal, whose old notice board is still conspicuous, was put up for public auction in 1878 and sold for the purposes of a mission hall.

The main building, whose lofty façade of brickwork we see from the road, is reached by a long tunnel-like corridor and well repays a visit of inspection, for happily but few structural alterations have been made since drama was banished from its stage

By 1879, largely through the efforts of Mr W. B. Redfern, Cambridge had once more an opportunity of witnessing plays. A disused skating rink in St Andrew's Street opposite the Police Station was acquired and fitted up as a theatre. The first of the series of Greek plays (the " Ajax ") was staged here in 1882, and theatrical performances were given more or less regularly until 1895, when the present New Theatre was built on the site of the old theatre or St Andrew's Hall, as it was at first called.

We are now within the precincts of the " pleasant little village of Barnwell," as this busy, squalid and crowded suburb was described by a writer at the end of the eighteenth century, and the little group

Barnwell, Cambridge.
W West

THE BIRD IN HAND INN.

of houses, then only some sixty-five in number, gathered round the old Abbey Church, well merited the description at that time. From the slight eminence above the river where it was pleasantly situated, there was nothing to obstruct the rural prospects commanded by the little village on every side ; to the south, beyond the common lands known as the Barnwell Fields an unbroken tract of fertile country stretched to the Gogmagog Hills ; to the north, a broad expanse of grass sloped down to Barnwell Pool ; and the church and cottages of Chesterton, well placed amidst gardens and trees on the opposite bank of the water, completed the pastoral scene.

Not far from the high road where we are now standing, and somewhere on the low ground towards the river, there existed in ancient times the lonely well from which the place takes its name. According to an account taken from an early chronicle relating to the Abbey this well appears to have consisted of several springs, and from the singular custom of children assembling there, on the eve of St John the Baptist, for games and merry-makings, the spot became known as the " Bairns' Well." Skeat emphatically denies this derivation of the word Barnwell, and states that the name signified " The Warrior's Well." However this may be, there seems no cause for doubting the truth of another legend, taken from the same source, concerning a hermit named Godesone, who is said to have built near the well and dedicated to St Andrew a little wooden oratory, where he ended his days in piety and peace. An ugly street in the neighbourhood (Godesdone Road) is labelled with the mis-spelt name of this holy man. It is, however, with the founding of its Priory that the true history of Barnwell begins, and we find ourselves dealing with reliable facts and dates.

Pain Peverel, a famous soldier who had been standard-bearer to Robert, Duke of Normandy during the first Crusade, was re-warded by the Barony and lands forfeited by the treasonable son of Picot, a former lord of Bourne and for many years sheriff of Cambridgeshire. Taking pity on the sad plight of the little Priory of St Giles by the Castle, founded in 1092 by Picot and Hugolina, his wife, for a prior and six canons regular of the Order of St Augustine, he resolved to remove and enlarge it so that the canons should equal in number the years of his age, namely thirty. To this end he obtained from Henry I. a grant of thirteen acres of land in Barnwell, between the high road and the river and including the Bairns' Well ; and there, not far from the little Oratory of St. Andrew, uncared for now owing to the hermit's recent death, he began to build in 1112, the new and greater Priory of St Giles and St Andrew.

Long before its great church, founded by Peverel and the first Prior, was completed, both were laid to rest within its walls, and it remained for the fifth Prior aided by the liberality of another wealthy and distinguished soldier, Everard de Beche, to finish the

THE CELLARER'S CHECKER, BARNWELL PRIORY.   Interior.

Face page 78

work. The name of Beche, like that of Godesone, has been bestowed on a local road.

In 1388 the Parliament of Cambridge is said to have assembled within the Priory, where Richard II. was lodged at the time. It was then that the " Statute of Cambridge," as it has been frequently termed, was passed, dealing with the cleansing of towns and throwing an interesting light on the state of filth then generally prevailing, the town of Cambridge being no exception to the rule.

Of this extensive, wealthy, and famous Priory nothing now remains save the railed-in fragment to be seen in Beche Road and the little thirteenth century church in Newmarket Road, commonly known as the Abbey Church ; the latter preserved because it was built for the use of the inhabitants dwelling outside the Priory Gate. Upon the dissolution of the Priory the building served as a convenient quarry. In 1578, when the Chapel of Corpus Christi College was being built, it is recorded that 182 loads of stone were removed from the dismantled monastery to the college. The priory grounds appear to have embraced the area extending from the site of Walnut Tree Avenue to that of River Lane, bounded as we have seen on the north by the river and on the south by the main road.

The houses clustering round the Priory Gate and Abbey Church grew in time into the pretty little village already described as being unspoiled at the end of the eighteenth century. But great changes were soon to take place. The passing of the Inclosure Act of 1807, followed by the Award of 20 April 1811, made possible the sale and cutting up of the open fields. A prodigious amount of speculative building began in response to the pressing need arising from the great influx of labour attracted to Cambridge by the extensions then being carried out by the colleges, and later supplemented by the large number of navvies engaged in making the Eastern Counties Railway. A network of streets arose as if by magic, the demand for houses continued, congestion and overcrowding followed, and soon the name of Barnwell acquired a notoriety which even now has not entirely passed away.

An unexpected feature of this suburb consists in the fact that it comprises inhabitants of three parishes, namely, Little St Andrew's

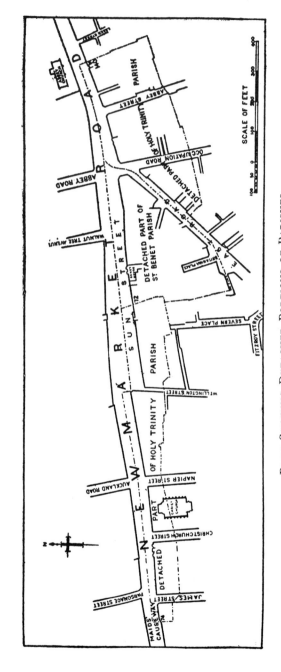

PLAN SHOWING DETACHED PORTIONS OF PARISHES.

(Barnwell), Holy Trinity, and St Bene't's. These detached pieces of parishes and their position far from their respective churches in the town are very curious and have been indicated upon the accompanying plan.

It is very difficult to account for their existence, but it would appear that the " Fields " and " Commons " surrounding the Town of Cambridge belonged to the community as a whole, irrespective of the different parishes of the place ; probably this was the case before the division of the town into separate parishes. Professor Maitland, in his *Township and Borough*, suggests that the application of the parochial system to the town-fields was gradual and fairly modern. If a strip of land in the " Fields " belonged to any parish at all, it would probably be reckoned as being in that parish to whose church it paid tithe. Maitland quotes the case of one " cultura " from different portions of which eight different churches took tithe ; there were frequent cases of adjoining strips paying tithe to different parishes. It is evident that, at the time of the enclosure, the " Fields " would have to be apportioned between the different parishes. It would be natural that the parishes in the outer ring should receive their allotments from the " Fields " already contiguous to them ; but parishes in the inner ring, that is to say in the centre of the town, would have their share in allotments of land quite detached from the actual parishes.

The broad open space intervening between the roadway and Sun Street was at one time used for that section of Midsummer Fair devoted to the sale of timber. At this great wood market everything could be purchased from the raw material down to hurdles, brushes and articles of turnery, and for a short period each summer, this far from beautiful spot presented a busy and picturesque scene.

Immediately facing Walnut Tree Avenue, formerly Midsummer Common Lane, on the site occupied by the premises adjoining the Sun Inn (now a private house, No. 94), was the original Barnwell Theatre, an inferior building opened in 1808 and soon superseded by another and greater Barnwell Theatre, namely, the Theatre Royal already referred to.

In connection with the Sun Inn the following tragic incident is recorded. It seems that a youth, aged between 16 and 18, who broke into this Inn and stole therefrom a silver spoon, was executed for theft on the 30 July 1786, at the Castle. We are told that " he behaved with decency, but testified the strongest intrepidity by taking the rope from the executioner, and, with amazing fortitude, throwing it over his head, and launching himself into eternity amidst the prayers and tears of an innumerable multitude."

Hard by, at the rear of Bene't House, was Warwicker's Yard, where on the 19 May 1829, the famous aeronaut, Mr Green, accompanied by two members of the University, ascended in a balloon. In the following May there were two ascents, in both cases students being carried as passengers, and for several years this yard each May witnessed all the excitement incident to the inflating of a balloon and its subsequent departure.

Retracing our steps for a few yards we come to the old battered Salmon publichouse, now a common lodging house. On the opposite side of the road another ancient and more picturesque inn is the Bird in Hand, one of the few old houses that has survived the ravages of time and fire. An eighteenth century writer tells us that

This village [Barnwell] hath often been reduced by fire but the last, which happened on September 30th, 1731, consumed a great part thereof. The fire was so very fierce that the engine which was carried thither to extinguish it was destroyed therewith ; for getting it into a farm yard, surrounded with houses and barns, the fire spread so fast that the people could scarcely get out without being burnt, nay, some were very much scorched in endeavouring to make their escape.[1]

At 67 Newmarket Road (near the Bird in Hand Inn) lived, during the last few years of his life, Dr George Cunningham, a remarkable man of wide interests and great ability, who became one of the greatest dental surgeons of his time. His report on the results of his investigations into the disease affecting workers in the match trade, known as " Phossy Jaw," undertaken at the request of the Government, has been described as " epoch-making." He devised a new system of preventing decay in the teeth of children

[1] Nichols' *Bibl. Topogr Brit.*, Vol. v., *Hist. of Barnwell Abbey*, p. 78.

which has been a source of great public benefit, and it was while he was lecturing on dentistry to the troops in France that he contracted his fatal illness, dying in London, 5 March 1919, with a world-wide reputation.

W. WEST.

1678

The Abbey House, Barnwell.

Dr Cunningham was an expert skater, and for many years no meeting of the National Skating Association was considered complete without him. He was something of a linguist, and found his knowledge of Esperanto of great value during his many travels.

At Newmarket Road, one large room served for him all the purposes of a home. It was a strange apartment containing a large open fire-place, with tapestry-covered walls, an assortment of furniture ranging from the Cromwellian to the Victorian period and filled with all kinds of trophies both of travel and the chase.

The Abbey House bears the date 1678 on one of its gables. To-day it presents a woeful appearance of neglect, though it is an interesting link with the later history of the Abbey Estate, before the property passed into the hands of the speculative builder in 1886.

This old red brick mansion was built by the Butler family, whose ancestor, Nevile Alexander Butler, acquired the Barnwell Abbey Estate in 1659, and was the first owner to reside thereon after the Dissolution. He appears to have revived an old custom dating back to the halcyon days of the suppressed Monastery, by entertaining each year on 16 June the Mayor and Corporation. In the quaint language of Alderman Newton's Diary we read that, on Monday, 14 June 1669 :

In the afternoone came Jo. Bridge the serjeant to me from Mr Mayor desiring my company at Mr Mayors house on Wednesday next betweene 12 and one of the clock in my Cloake to accompany him to Mr Butler's at Barnewell, as yearely the custome is.

Wednesday betweene 1 and 2 met the Aldermen . . . at Mr Mayors house with the Treasurers old and new elect, the Bayliffs and severall of the 24ty[1] from whence the Mayor in his Gowne with Marsh the Serjeant in his Gowne and with the mace, before the Mayor, the Aldermen and rest in their Cloakes went to Barnwell Abbey to Mr Butlers who complimented us and afterwards Mrs Butler came whom the Mayor and Aldermen onely saluted; there at Mr. Butlers charge all the company had Gamon of Bacon, cream, and stewed pruens and strong beere and cake and the Towne sent wine and sugar and soe after the Treat done the company went away from thence. . . .

Jacob, Alexander's grandson, and successor to the property in 1714, known in Barnwell history as Squire Butler, was one of the most extraordinary characters ever known in these parts. This wrong-headed, eccentric, litigious but not unkindly personage was a graduate of the University, and at the time of his death in 1765,

[1] The twenty-four members of the Council were commonly called at this period *The Twenty-fourty*.

SQUIRE BUTLER, from an etching by Michael Tyson, reproduced
from Nichols' *Bibl. Top. Brit.* Vol. V.

at the age of 84, was the oldest Barrister in England. The Squire was six feet four inches high, and the Rev. Michael Tyson, of Corpus Christi College, has left an admirable etching of his striking features as they appeared in crusty old age. According to his own account :

> He feared his God ;
> He honoured his King ;
> He despised his foes,
> And valued his friends.[1]

The following particulars of this remarkable man are taken from a rare little octavo volume containing the History of Barnwell[2]:

His coffin, which was made from a large oak by his express order, some months before his death, became an object of public curiosity ; it was of sufficient dimensions to contain several persons, and wine was copiously quaffed therein by many of those who went to see it. To . . . one of the Legatees, the singular trust was delegated of driving him to the grave, on the carriage of a waggon, divested of the body ; seated in the front, he was to drive his two favourite horses, Brag and Dragon, to Barnwell Church, and should they refuse to receive his body there, he was to return and bury him in the middle of the grass-plat in his own garden ; part only of his request was complied with. . . . The loss of a favourite dog, about two months before his death, is supposed to have accelerated his end ; upon this event being announced to him, he explained " I shall not live long, now my dog is dead ! " From that instant he was taken ill, and never recovered.

Mr Butler, having obtained a suit at law, which if he had lost would have ruined him, caused the following lines to be inscribed on his carriage :

> Cambridge to wit ;
> The biter is bit :
> I will magnity thee, O Lord,
> For you have set me up.

As owner of Stourbridge Fair field :

He was very rigid in seeing the Cherter of the Fair complied with, for if the ground was not cleared by one o'clock on the day appointed (if any booths, etc., were standing), he had them pulled down and took the materials away. One day he drove his carriage amongst the crockery-ware, and destroyed

[1] Nichols' *Bibl. Topogr. Brit.*, Vol. v., *Hist. of Barnwell Abbey*, . . . *Appendix*, p. 8.
[2] This has no title page, but the first page is headed *The History and Antiquities, etc., Barnwell Abbey*, and is almost entirely taken from Nichols. The volume does not appear in the British Museum catalogue, nor in the catalogue of the Cambridge University Library, and I can only presume that it was privately printed, and only a very few copies issued. The date of the volume is *c.* 1830.

a great quantity of it, because the ground was not cleared at the time mentioned in the Charter. The giants and dwarfs, who came for exhibition at the Fair, were usually invited to dine with him.

Against the western wall of the Abbey church-yard stand six slate slabs, three commemorative of Squire Butler's ancestors and relatives, and three autobiographical. Originally fixed as mural tablets in the Chancel, they have long occupied their present position where the elements are fast helping to soften the bitterness of the words inscribed upon them by this stubborn and much persecuted worthy.

The following ghost story connected with this old house is unusually curious, since the ghost was only apparent to certain children.

It seems that early in the present century there was living at the Abbey House a family whose younger members were wont to see, during their play, a diminuitive hairy creature stalk slowly across the room. The children aptly referred to their strange visitor as Furrey. So familiar had Furrey's visits to their play-room become that they excited no unusual interest beyond the curious fact that their brother Arnold could never see Furrey even when his attention was directed to it by his brothers and sisters, and it was only this lack of recognition by Arnold that puzzled their minds.

Perhaps in Furrey we have the wandering shade of Squire Butler's favourite dog restlessly seeking the spirit of his beloved master in their old home !

We must not leave the church-yard without devoting a few moments to the old church itself. It is a little Early English building some 70 feet long and 18 feet wide without aisles, and still dimly lighted by its original lancet windows. Among later insertions, the Perpendicular window on the south is worthy of notice. From Bowtell's MSS. we learn that near the pulpit, in 1811, there was an iron stand for an hour-glass which, from the Church accounts, Bowtell adds, appears to have been fixed there as early as 1560. The rood screen richly carved, coloured, and gilt, was remaining as late as 1826. In 1846, the building, having become very dilapidated, was closed, but in 1854 it was put in thorough repair and re-opened once more for Divine Service in 1856.

Opposite is Leeke Street, and at the corner of this little street bearing the surname of a former Vicar of the parish, stands the old Mendicity House once a " superior " common lodging-house, super-vised and supported by a local charitable institution known as the Mendicity Society.

Resuming our journey we soon reach the large farm-yard and premises facing Godesdone Road, where some years ago was situated a Chicory-malting establishment.

On the same side of the road is the Racehorse Inn. " Here the cheese fair began," writes Gunning in 1789, and :

From thence till you came opposite the road leading to Chesterton Ferry, the ground was exclusively occupied by dealers in that article. It was the great mart at which all the dealers in cheese from Cottenham, Willingham, and other villages in the county and isle assembled ; there were also traders from Leicestershire, Derbyshire, Cheshire, and Gloucestershire.

Our walk now brings us to a terrace of houses known as Shakes-peare Cottages. These occupy the site on which once stood a roomy timber building used as a theatre during the period of Stour-bridge Fair, and described on the play-bills before me as " Stirbitch Theatre."

Pursuing our way to more agreeable and open surroundings we come in due time to Garlic Row, and turning down this bare and wind-swept road soon reach an old and solitary house, partly rebuilt and bearing under its eaves, in iron letters, the name, " J. LEE," and on a stone over the doorway, the date, " 1707." This is said to have been used as a Court House during Stourbridge Fair, and was for long noted as an oyster-house—tons of oyster-shells have been exhumed on the adjoining War Allotments !

For an account of the association of this house with the ceremony of proclaiming the fair, we cannot do better than turn to the pages of Gunning :

The proclamation was read by the Registrary in the carriage with the Vice-Chancellor. . . At the conclusion of this ceremony the carriages drew up at the Tiled Booth (which is still standing), where the company alighted for the dispatch of business—and of oysters ; and passing through an upper room . . . they at length arrived at what was called " The University Dining

Room." . . . Close to the end wall was a narrow bench ; next that, the table, formed from rough materials, and supported by tressels and casks ; on this table (which had no cloth of any kind) were placed several barrels of oysters, with ale and bottled porter in great profusion. . . . We then left the dining-room that the waiters might remove the shells and cover the boards with a cloth, in preparation for dinner. . . . We took two or three turns in Garlick-row, and then returned to the Tiled Booth. . . . Before the Vice-Chancellor was placed a large dish of herrings, then followed in order, a neck of pork roasted, an enormous plum-pudding, a leg of pork boiled, a pease-pudding, a goose, a huge apple-pie, and a round of beef in the centre.   On the other half of the table the same dishes were placed in similar order (the herrings before the Senior Proctor, who sat at the bottom).   From thirty to forty persons dined there, and although the wine was execrable a number of toasts were given, and mirth and good humour prevailed, to such an extent as is seldom to be met with at more modern and more refined entertainments.   At about half-past six the dinner party broke up, and, with scarcely an exception, adjourned to the theatre.

But the chief interest of the old house lies in the fact that it marks the site of the fair, which covered an area of about half a mile square.

Defoe[1] has left us a graphic account of this great European mart as it existed when he visited it in the eighteenth century, and has detailed the enormous business transacted during its three weeks' duration, the pages of Defoe are easily accessible and have been so freely quoted by many writers that we need not do more than note very briefly its origin, rise and decay.

The origin of this celebrated fair is lost in obscurity.   No charter appears to exist, but history records the granting of the fair by King John, about the year 1211, for the benefit of the adjoining Hospital for Lepers, though there is no doubt that it was then already well established.   Its situation on the river, more easily navigable from the coast before the fens were drained, doubtless explains its early importance as an inland centre of distribution for sea-borne goods ; conversely, as the banks of the river became more restricted and better and other more convenient means of transport were introduced, its relative importance gradually declined.

It has been suggested that to Bunyan, Stourbridge Fair, served as the prototype for his " Vanity Fair," his recollections of visits as

[1] *A tour through the whole island of Great Britain.*   4th ed. 1748, Vol. I, p. 91 *et seq.*

a lad being depicted in those vivid touches of the lighter and darker sides of the bustling scenes witnessed in his youth. Another great name associated with this fair is that of Isaac Newton, of whom it is recorded that he there bought his famous prism.

Crossing by the railway-bridge, we come to a little wicket-gate leading to the Chapel of the Hospital for Lepers, dedicated to St Mary Magdalene, where we may well pause and muse awhile upon the nine-hundred-years-old memorial before us, impressive in its Norman simplicity, and ponder upon the probable boundaries of the long vanished buildings of the Hospice that once sheltered these poor outcasts of society and the site of their forgotten burying-ground. During the latter period of the late War, this Chapel was utilised as a Garrison Church for the patients of a temporary military isolation hospital set up in the neighbourhood, and so, for a second time in its long history, it afforded consolation to afflicted humanity.

At the foot of the bridge stands an antiquated Toll-house, a relic of those old Coaching-days when a journey by road was often enlivened by an adventure with highwaymen.

In 1817 a farmer of Little Wilbraham was riding home from Cambridge market, when he was attacked and robbed of nearly £100 on the very outskirts of the town, in fact not far from Alderman Burleigh's house.[1] Even with the advent of the railway and the decline of coaching, the belated traveller was not entirely safe from these pests of the road as the following story shows :

During the afternoon of Wednesday last, Mrs Page, who with her daughters keeps the toll-house on the Paper-Mills road, noticed two or three suspicious characters lurking about, and as they did not withdraw as night fell she mentioned her uneasiness to two gentlemen who passed the gate on their way to Bottisham. They made light of the matter, saying the men no doubt were anxious to keep near shelter from the impending storm. Partly to allay her fears, and partly for the last mentioned reason, they waited till the storm had subsided, and then deparetd on their way. All remained quiet until between one and two o'clock in the morning of Thursday, when (just after the passage of the mail cart) a lusty cry of " gate " was heard, and Mrs Page proceeded to open it, but was advised not to do so by her second daughter, who remarked that she heard no sound of horses. Mrs Page waited until her daughter had

[1] *Cambridge Chronicle*, 26 September 1817.

armed herself with a loaded pistol, and then carefully opened the door, which was a common one, opening inwards with a hutch door opening the reverse way. The inner door was no sooner open than a tall man thrust a stick in, and made a blow at Mrs Page's head, but fortunately missed his aim, and the blow fell on her breast, hurting her but slightly. The door was slammed to by Mrs Page, and a scuffle ensued, the robber trying to make good his entry with his stick, which was jammed in the doorway. Miss Page was assisting to keep the door close, and had dropped the first pistol. She motioned to her sister to give her a second, which was lying on the table. Her sister complied and then taking aim in the direction in which the stick indicated that the assailant was standing, fired. She heard an exclamation of " Oh ! " as though the man was hit, and immediately the sounds of retreating footsteps of two or three persons. Miss Page then opened the door and fired the second pistol. The stick was left behind. The mailman states that when he passed he saw two men standing under the adjacent trees as though for shelter. The courage of Miss Page is the theme of universal admiration. There seems to be but little doubt that the man was hit, though it is not probable he was dangerously hurt, as the pistol was a small one, and loaded with small shot.[1]

A few yards further along the Newmarket Road bring us to a neighbourhood known as The Paper Mills, and in this connection we may quote Fuller's observations upon the passing of an old industry in Cambridgeshire :

Paper is entred as a Manufacture of this County, because there are Mills, nigh Sturbridge-fair, where Paper was made in the memory of our Fathers. And it seemeth to me a proper Conjunction, that seeing Cambridge yieldeth so many good writers, Cambridgeshire should afford Paper, unto them. Pitty, the making thereof is disused : considering the vast sums yearly expended in our Land for Paper out of Italy, France and Germany, which might be lessened were it made in our Nation. To such who object that we can never equall the perfection of Venice paper, I return, neither can we match the purity of Venice-glasses, and yet many green ones are blown in Sussex, profitable to the makers and convenient for the users thereof, as no doubt such courser (home-spun-Paper) would be found very beneficial for the Common-wealth.[2]

It is interesting to find that although the manufacture of paper here had already ceased as far back as the early part of the seventeenth century, yet the memory of its past association with this locality has survived, being, until recently, commemorated by an Inn, now better known, however, under its present title of The Globe, and also by the long forsaken tea-gardens on the other side of the

---

[1] *Cambridge Chronicle*, 5 May 1849.   [2] Fuller, *Worthies*, 1662, p. 149.

road, now used as a builder's store-yard. In our quest for the site of the mill-wheel, we must seek admittance to the delightful garden attached to the picturesque gabled house adjoining The Globe,

W. West.

The Moat, formerly known as Paper Mills.

named The Moat, where may be seen the old mill race and the clear and sparkling brook rushing down to the river below. In more recent times the old building appears to have been used as a flour-mill, but owing to operations undertaken by the Waterworks Company at Cherryhinton, the supply of water was so seriously lessened as to render the water-wheel useless, when the Company, in order to avoid litigation, acquired the freehold.

In our earlier walks it may be recalled we noticed under the eaves of several old houses three or four iron rings. The Globe Inn presents another example of these curious appendages.

The
Globe Inn
Fen Ditton,
Cambs.

W. West.

Having obtained permission to pass through a modern gateway across the road, we soon find ourselves beneath a rusty arch of ironwork surmounted by a broken lamp, gazing upon the once famous but now deserted tea-gardens. Here was a spacious lawn surrounded by picturesque tea-houses and shaded by lofty trees, where our grandfathers came to play bowls and skittles ; and here, when the shades of evening fell and festoons of flickering lamps stretched from branch to branch, lovers walked beside the dark mill-stream and dancers tripped merrily upon the green-sward to the strains of harp and fiddle. Nothing now remains save an array of derelict wooden sheds filled with builder's stores and a barren tract of ground where a few broken bushes and tufts of rank grass struggle for existence amidst stacks of bricks and little mountains of lime.

Leaving this melancholy spot and regaining the high road we find ourselves close to Ditton Lane and the open country, and realise that we have passed the borough boundary and so have brought our fourth and last walk through the town to an end. Although this walk has been taken, for the most part, through an unlovely and apparently uninteresting district, it has proved to be singularly fruitful in memories of the past and in glimpses of the Cambridge of a remote age.

As we wend our way homewards through the slums of Barnwell, after recalling these sights and scenes of antiquity, it is difficult to contemplate without anxiety the headlong rush after amusement and gain characteristic of to-day; and we cannot look back without regret to the simple life of those good old times when young Cambridge practised archery upon Butt's Green; when children, on Midsummer Eve, danced innocently and happily round the holy well; and when, with the pale curling smoke of his evening fire, the hermit's prayer rose to heaven from his lonely cell.

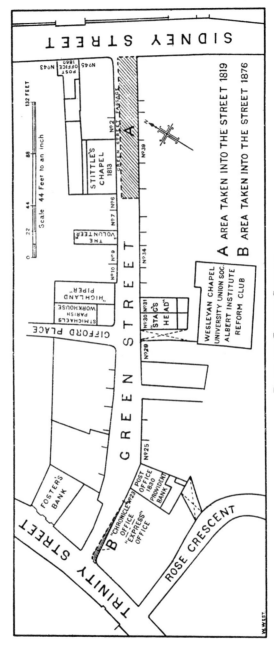

SIDNEY STREET

POST OFFICE No.45 1860

No.43

STITTLE'S CHAPEL 1813

No.2

132 FEET

88   44

Scale 44 Feet to an inch

22   44

0

No.39

THE VOLUNTEER

No.7 No.6

GREEN STREET

ST.MARY'S PASSAGE

No.10

No.34

GIFFORD PLACE

"HIGHLAND PIPER"

ST.MICHAELS PARISH WORKHOUSE

No.30 No.31

STAG'S HEAD

No.28

WESLEYAN CHAPEL UNIVERSITY UNION SOC. ALBERT INSTITUTE REFORM CLUB

No.25

FOSTER'S BANK

"CHRONICLE" No.23 OFFICE "EXPRESS" OFFICE

POST OFFICE 1830 PROVIDENT BANK

B

TRINITY STREET

ROSE CRESCENT

W.W.1ST.

A AREA TAKEN INTO THE STREET 1819
B AREA TAKEN INTO THE STREET 1876

PLAN OF GREEN STREET.

CHAPTER V.

Green Street : To-day and Yesterday[1]

T first sight, it must be confessed, there is little in the Green Street of to-day to inspire the antiquary or attract the traveller.

An air of comfortable and placid respectability reminiscent of better days distinguished until recently this narrow but convenient bye-way between Sidney Street and Trinity Street, but now even this has vanished, and nowhere else in Cambridge is there more visible evidence of the economic effects of war.

Its undergraduate population knows it no more, its busy colony of lodging-house keepers have long since fled, the curtainless windows of forsaken rooms stare empty-eyed at the furtive passer-by, while two gaunt and tenantless houses tower conspicuously above the rest, their crumbling brickwork breaking away as though in utter weariness of standing sentinel so long and uncared for amidst the surrounding desolation.

Here, too, at night the enforced darkness of the town seems to assume a more impenetrable gloom, and the death-like stillness is but occasionally broken by the sound of hesitating steps upon the pavement.

At times, indeed, the old street assumes a grim but fitful gaiety, for the billeting officers find in its dismantled buildings ample accommodation for their men during their transient stay in the town. Then sharp, staccato commands ring out to the sound of military

[1] This chapter originally appeared in the *Cambridge Chronicle* and the *Cambridge Daily News* during the Great War (17 April 1916).

95

tramping, baggage waggons obstruct the road, and the strains of " Tipperary " echo through some peaceful student's forsaken abode.

But let us leave this melancholy spectacle for the Green Street of yesterday. Its memories, its close association with University and civic life yield many interesting facts and connections.

Green Street, in the days of its prosperity, was one of the liveliest parts of the town. Important buildings, both civil and religious, lay within its precincts and the busy yards of three popular inns opened upon its narrow way. Here also was situated St Michael's parish pump, which was stolen and carried away bodily in 1816, causing the annoyed churchwardens to offer no less a sum than £10 for the apprehension of the delinquents !

Until 1819 the only access into Sidney Street lay through Green Street Passage, a narrow footway 120 feet long, which gave our thoroughfare the shape of a bottle-neck.

From Bowtell's *History of the Town* we learn that the old name of Green Street was Highe Warde Lane, and that of the passage Burden Hostel Lane, from the fact that it led in earlier days to Burden Hostel, which occupied a site extending from Messrs. Macintosh's yard to a frontage facing Trinity Lane.

The street takes its present name from Oliver Green, M.D. (1563-1623), of Caius College, who was a man of property and a native of Trumpington. Willis and Clark, in their *Architectural History of the University* (Vol. I., page 183), quoting from the *Annals* of Dr Caius, state that in 1614, on the occasion of the visit of King James, Green voluntarily undertook to repair the College sundials at the Gate of Honour and elsewhere, and " that on this gentleman's estate, the street, which from his name is called Green Street, had been recently erected." From this we may infer that Highe Warde Lane first became lined by houses and so rose to the dignity of a street, in the early years of the seventeenth century.

The religious memories of Green Street are confined to the Nonconformist movement, which owes so much to the influence of that remarkable Puritan, Francis Holcroft, Fellow of Clare and Vicar of Bassingbourne, known as the Apostle of Cambridgeshire, who suffered imprisonment for his opinions in Cambridge Castle, and, dying in 1693, was buried near his colleague, Joseph Oddy, in a plot of land he had purchased as a Nonconformist burial ground,

The Revᵈ John Stittle
of Green Street Meeting-house, Cambridge

now a garden adjoining the churchyard at Oakington, where his tomb may still be seen.

On the site of the houses numbered 5, 4, and 3 stood an old Independent Chapel, dating back to 1688, generally known as the Old Green Street Meeting House, but in later days often referred to with less respect as Stittle's Chapel, after the Rev. John Stittle, who served his congregation here from his appointment in 1781 until his death.

John Stittle (miscalled " Stettle " by Byron in 1811 in the *Hints from Horace*), was born at Madingley in 1727, and died in 1813. He was one of the many Cambridgeshire converts won to piety by that eccentric clergyman, John Berridge, the friend of Wesley He was a hedger and a thrasher, could read well, but never could write. This had the advantage of compelling him to preach extempore ; (and some people are said to wish, for the sake of the same advantage, that all preachers were blind). An anecdote, which Professor de Morgan has immortalised, represents him as saying, in contempt of academical learning, " D'ye think Powle (*i.e.* St Paul) knew Greek ? " But Professor Adam Sedgwick, the eminent geologist, declared this anecdote quite incredible, and utterly at variance with the strong mental powers which Stittle possessed. When Mr Simeon, who had befriended Stittle, preached a University sermon, in which he stated Calvinism more moderately than had been usual with him, some of those Dissenters who had occasionally attended his church became offended at his apparent change of views, and consequently transferred themselves altogether to Stittle's chapel. Simeon, nevertheless, did not resent this, and ultimately he very generously made Stittle a permanent quarterly allowance, which, he jocularly said, was " for shepherding my stray sheep." (The tradition of this saying was preserved by a person who had often been employed by Simeon to carry the money.) Stittle remained to the end a high Calvinist. He used to say, " Arminians are like wood-pigeons. They say ' Do, do, do ' all day long, but they are the laziest birds that fly." He would have sympathised with the poet who wrote :

' Go search Paul's Epistles, you shallow Arminians,
You'll not find one text to support your opinions.'

He rejected all water baptism, either of infants or adults. He had a standing feud with the undergraduates. They used, as Byron suggests, to go to Greenstreet to ridicule the sermons, and would bring sparrows into the chapel and let them loose. One man, seeing himself watched, put his cap in front of his face, upon which Stittle grimly observed, " In the Day of Judgment there'll be no caps to hide your face in." In old age he used to be carried to the chapel in a Sedan chair. An undergraduate called out to the bearers as they were carrying Stittle over Magdalene Bridge, from Castle End, where he lived, " Drop him over the bridge into hell." Stittle replied, " They can't, for my Master keeps the keys of hell." One day he was met in Petty Cury by three undergraduates, who respectively accosted him, the one as " Father Abraham," the next as " Father Isaac," and the third as " Father Jacob." He replied, " I am none of the three, I am merely Saul, son of Kish, sent to seek my father's asses. And lo ! *I have found them.*" He preached so long a series of sermons on David, that one of his flock complained, " You have picked all the flesh off David's bones." He replied, " Yes, and I shall now crack the bones and see what marrow is in them." In one sermon he compared eternity to a clock so gigantic that it said " tic " in one century and " tac " in the next. Then suddenly turning to some undergraduates in the chapel he said : " Go home and calculate the length of that clock's pendulum." On one occasion when insulted by undergraduates he invited one of them to come to his house and share the " herby pie " supper of his family ; after which he induced him to stay on for family worship ; this resulted in the youth being led to think seriously of religion, and in his ultimately becoming a valuable clergyman. Stittle was four times married, and survived his fourth wife. He said that if he had known that he should survive her so many years he would have married a fifth one. (But he had not the foresight of the man who engraved on the wedding ring of the fourth wife, " If I survive I'll make them five.")

In Dean Alford's *Plea for the Queen's English* there is given a powerful passage from one of Stittle's sermons. He died in 1813, aged 85.[1]

It was once the custom in certain Nonconformist places of worship to erect a special pew to contain the Communion table, and it was beneath such a table pew, as it was called, that this zealous minister was buried amidst the scene of his former labours. His remains were subsequently removed to Eden Street Chapel, where in the lobby a tablet records his thirty years of faithful ministry in Green Street. His body, it is said, was found in perfect preservation, but in a few minutes it fell to dust, leaving only the skeleton to be re-interred.

We may take leave of this extraordinary character with the following extract from one of his many homely sermons—quoted often by my grandmother—that seems applicable in these present days of enforced economy : " One egg makes a good pudding, two an excellent one, three is an extravagance, but four eggs in a pudding is an abomination before the Lord ! "

The building now numbered 30 and 31 was in those days the Stag's Head Inn, and under its once busy covered way—now the approach to Thurston's Billiard Rooms—passed our Wesleyan forebears to service at yet another place of worship in its rear ;

[1] I am greatly indebted to Dr Courtney Kenny for permission to reprint the above account of this remarkable man, which appeared in an article entitled *A Forgotten Cambridge-Meeting House*, published in the *Cambridge Independent Press* many years ago.

A DEBATE at the UNION.

The Old Union Debating House, from *A Cambridge Scrap Book*.

from the following notice in the *Cambridge Chronicle* of 16 April, 1819, we learn the date of the present building :

> The New Chapel
> In Green Street, Cambridge,
> Will be opened on Tuesday next,
> the 29th inst., when Three Sermons
> will be preached by the Rev. John
> Hyatt, of London, and others. The
> Service in the morning will commence
> at half-past Ten o'clock,
> after which further notice will be given.

In 1850 the congregation migrated to their newly-built chapel in Hobson Street, upon the site of which now stands the present County Hall.

The empty chapel was taken over in the same year (1850) by the University Union Society, and remained in their occupation till 1866 ; a view of their " dingy old room in Green Street "—as the late Professor Fawcett called it on one occasion—may be seen in *A Cambridge Scrap-Book*, published by Messrs. Macmillan & Co. in 1859, in a sketch entitled " A Debate at the Union."

When the Union Society moved elsewhere the unexpired lease of the property was taken over by Ernest Boys, a Rustat Scholar of Jesus College who, with other earnest believers in muscular Christianity, had formed in the previous year (1 May 1865) the Albert Institute.

This was a social club having for its objects the promotion of religious instruction and healthy recreation among the young men of the town, providing for them a library, reading-room, evening classes and lectures and, incidentally, forming a bureau for obtaining employment.

Mr Gerard Cobb, the composer of " Mandalay," took charge for a time of the musical side of the Club, whilst the Rev. Charles Kingsley, Dr Westcott, afterwards Bishop of Durham, and Dr H. R. Luard, amongst others, gave lectures to the members.

But, excellent though it was, the Club did not long survive the departure from Cambridge of its enthusiastic president, and soon afterwards we find the premises in the occupation of the Reform Club.

This was a political Society holding radical views considered extreme in their day, and the fact that their headquarters had a northern aspect gave the local Tory paper an excuse for alluding to its members as " our friends on the *shady* side of Green Street."

Messrs. Macintosh's yard was, in the old coaching days, the busy stable-yard approach to the Angel Inn, whose imposing frontage faced the Market Hill, next door to the once famous Rose and Crown, commemorated in Rose Crescent, where from its balcony —still to be seen over Messrs. Reed's shop—fervid orations were poured forth at election times.

In the early part of the 19th century the Post Office was situated at 24, Green Street, the Postmaster being Mr James Brown, father of Mr Charles Edward Brown sometime connected with the *Cambridge Chronicle*, and Mayor of the Borough in 1846-7 and 1868-9. The position of the Post Office is shown on Baker's map of Cambridge published in 1830.

Here, at No. 24, the business of the Provident Bank was also transacted for many years by Mr Brown; the Savings Bank, as it was latterly called, subsequently out-grew its office accommodation, and more suitable buildings were erected in Sidney Street, which are now known as Bank Chambers.

The quaint old house numbered 23 is a typical specimen of many of the old houses once seen in the street ; adjoining, and extending into Trinity Street, stood the picturesque old printing offices of the *Cambridge Chronicle*. Upon removal, in 1836, to their present quarters on the Market Hill, Messrs. Metcalfe and Palmer took over the premises, and here, in the autumn of 1868, the *Cambridge Express* first saw the light. With the demolition of the old property in 1876, the opportunity was taken to add about five feet to the narrow entrance into Trinity Street.

Gifford Place takes its name from the residence of Alderman James Gifford (died 1774), whose old Georgian building of red brick,

OAK-PANELLED ROOM, FORMERLY PART OF THE ANGEL INN.
(In the yard of Messrs. Macintosh & Sons.)

Face page 102

OLD HOUSES IN GREEN STREET, probably part of Burden's Hostel; from a photograph by J. Palmer Clarke.

Face page 103

standing in retiring dignity well back from its lofty entrance gates has been demolished, and its site absorbed by recent extensions of the business premises of a later-day Alderman of the Borough.

Lazarus-like at the entrance-gate was the Parish Poorhouse, a building which still exists, in outward appearance, much as it did in those sad bygone days, of which it stands a pathetic record.

At the left corner of Gifford Place was established in 1784 the gun-making firm of William Gallyon. On the site of the old premises the present house (No. 14) was built by the family about 1832, not long before the business was transferred to its present address in Bridge Street.

Towards the end of the 18th century flourished somewhere in this street the book-binding establishment of John Bowtell, nephew of his more distinguished namesake, the bookbinder, antiquary, and benefactor of Addenbrooke's Hospital and other local charities.

Until the middle of the last century, on the site of the house at the right-hand entrance to Gifford Place, stood two old weather-beaten tenements numbered respectively 12 and 11, the latter a beer-house called the Highland Piper, approached by brick steps leading down to its entrance door.

The year 1849 may be still remembered locally in connexion with the fire at St Michael's. It was about half-past ten on the morning of Sunday, 11 November, that the good folk of Green Street and its immediate neighbourhood first heard that their Parish Church was on fire.

Those were the days of manual fire-engines, and street hydrants were unknown. The problem of supplying water to the five engines that were quickly on the scene was solved by forming a double line of willing helpers to Trinity kitchen ; on one side the empty buckets were passed down to the college pump, on the other they were whirled at the rate of six miles an hour from the hands of one to the other when replenished.

Soon the supply of water from the kitchens began to fail, the lines of water carriers were then extended through the New Court

THE FIRE AT ST MICHAEL'S CHURCH, from *The Illustrated London News*, 17 Nov. 1849.

ST MICHAEL's WORKHOUSE.

Face page 104

down to the river and two hours passed before the fire was got under. The outbreak appears to have originated in the church flues and thence to have spread to the roof of the south aisle.

The *Illustrated London News* of 17 November 1849, shows the church in full blaze, and to judge by the vivid illustration the efforts to subdue the fire appear to be confined entirely to members of the University, who in cap and gown are show working the engines, whilst others, also in correct academical attire, are seen on the roof with lengths of hose, endeavouring to quench the flames.

Numbers 10, 9, and 8 are now the only early eighteenth century houses left on the north side of Green Street, number 8, now The Volunteer, being notable as the former home of a worthy barber named Crowson, once renowned far and wide for his excellent Bear's-grease, who, as an indisputable testimony to the genuineness of the said article, for long imprisoned in his cellar a bear. On fine days the poor brute would seek " a place in the sun " by climbing up on to the roomy ledge in its ample area, to the great delight and wonderment of the juvenile inhabitants of the neighbourhood.

An old friend and native of Green Street who recollects the bear, tells me it was also shown at times in a back room behind an iron grating. The unfortunate animal having become more dangerous than attractive, was eventually shot, when portions of it were cut up into hams and steaks and distributed among various customers.

From the same source I learn that two inhabitants who flourished at about the same period as the bear were dwarfs, neither of them standing over four feet high, and both notable characters. One of these little men was an undertaker, living at No. 34, who much accentuated his quaint appearance by wearing a coat of blue with brass buttons, surmounted by a top hat. The other, who lived in a house in Messrs. Macintosh's yard, divided his attention between the law and the turf. The puny form and enormous white hat of this diminutive attorney rendered him a conspicuous object on Newmarket Heath, whilst his neighbours in Green Street looked upon him as a veritable prototype of Quilp.

The tragic death in the Soudan in 1882 of Edward Henry Palmer, Lord Almoner's Professor of Arabic in the University, has already been referred to, but it is probably known to few that Palmer was born in Green Street (1840). An excellent portrait of this distinguished orientalist, in eastern costume, hangs in the dining hall of St John's College.

Another native of Green Street was the late Mr Joseph Prior, who was tutor to the Duke of Clarence during his residence at Trinity College as an undergraduate.

Before leaving the old street, two other links with the past remain to be noticed. The eighteenth century bakehouse at No. 9 still produces its daily batch of bread, and, still is heard the melancholy tap-tap of the bookbinder's hammer, reminding us of a craft for which Cambridge has ever been famous, and awakening, at the same time, echoes and memories of bygone days of prosperity and peace.

CHAPTER VI.

The Great Cambridge Fire of 1849

AMBRIDGE can show few livelier prospects than her Market-place as seen on some sunny Saturday in early summer. The spacious square and tall church tower, the wide array of canvas-covered booths, the blocked streets, and the gay and good-humoured throng crowding through every available space amidst shouting hawkers, heaped-up flower-stalls, pyramids of country produce and the decrepit vans of village carriers, form a scene which for brilliance and vivacity, recalls rather the air of a continental town than that of the seat of a sober English University. Yet few, perhaps, realise that the fine Market Square we know to-day is of comparatively recent origin, or can remember the great conflagration which brought it into being.

Before, however, proceeding to a description of the most famous of Cambridge fires, it will be well to glance very briefly at the site of the Market-place as it appeared in early times.

As will be seen from the accompanying plan[1]. the original " Market-hill " was little more than a wide street traversing the eastern side of the site, between Market-street and Petty Cury, whilst at right angles to it lay a somewhat larger area connecting Petty Cury with the northern end of Peas Hill, and known as Market Ward.

The rest of the square was occupied by a large block of irregular houses clustered together like a rookery, extending as far south as the present railings of St Mary's Passage and nearly as far east as Rose Crescent, whilst its upper or western part overflowed into St Mary's Churchyard, certain portions being actually built against the chancel itself, so that, it has been gravely stated, worshippers within could obtain an excellent view of the interior of an adjoining

---

[1] Drawn by my son, Capt. Arthur J. Gray, when on the Ypres Salient in 1916, from information supplied by me.   A.B.G.

bedroom. This mass of buildings was divided from north to south by a very narrow thoroughfare, known latterly as Warwick-street, and in earlier times nicknamed Pump-lane, from the most conspicuous feature standing in its midst. Opposite the old pump, and with its back premises touching the church, stood the noted public house of Messrs. Ind, known as The Grapes, and said to have been the origin of the great Burton firm of Ind, Coope and Co.

The S.W. corner of the present Market-place is approximately the spot where once stood the Market Cross, in the centre of the area then called, from the character of the produce sold upon it, the Green Hill. What visions of our civic life and national history are awakened by the thought of that Market Cross! From its steps what Royal Proclamations have been read by past generations of Mayors and Town Clerks, in all the setting of civic dignity and popular acclamation! An extract from the diary of Alderman Newton, dated 18 February 1688, tells us of the ceremony of proclaiming King William III. and Queen Mary:

. . . the Maior and Aldermen arrived in Scarlett on horseback and the Common Counsill on horseback in their Gownes with many that had past offices and other Freeman, first they were proclaimed at the Market Crosse, 2ly on the market place on the Hill neare the Rose Taverne, . . .

Regrettable as it was that the Town Council in 1786 thought fit to destroy the old Market Cross, it is at least interesting to remember that its site is still perpetuated, for it is here that all Royal Proclamations are first read, the second declaration being made, as in Alderman Newton's day, at the corner of the Hill nearest Rose-crescent.

Until 1842, the year when the Corn Exchange was built on St Andrew's Hill, the corn market was held between Market Street and Rose Crescent, and here, during the first half of the last century, might have been seen on market days a venerable member of our University in academical dress, bargaining with farmers and exhibiting his sample-bags of grain. This keen agriculturist was Dr Webb, Master of Clare Hall (1815-1856), and a past master in the breeding of pigs, and of his dealings in them many good stories have been told. One story goes that, while proceeding with an equally

ENTRANCE TO PUMP LANE, from a water-colour by Samuel Oliver, dated 1850, now in the Cambridge Free Library.

MARKET HILL IN 1801, looking south, from a drawing by Rowlandson in the Cambridge Free Library.

Face page 109

bucolic companion to attend a University sermon, the Reverend Doctor had an animated discussion with his friend upon the respective merits of the various breeds of pigs, and it was not until they found themselves entering the precincts of St Mary's Church that this absorbing conversation was terminated by the Doctor emphatically asserting in a loud whisper that nothing came up to the blue-arse pig !

Dr Webb is gratefully remembered for the unique collection of University papers which he gathered during his mastership, and which is now in the University Library. It was not until 1870, when the *University Reporter* first appeared, that the University had any official medium for publishing the various edicts, graces of the Senate, reports, etc.

Not far from the Cross and opposite to the site of the present Guildhall stood the old Hobson's Conduit, surrounded by an iron palisade. It has been recorded that it was the custom to secure to these railings the culprits condemned to a public whipping. With the completion of the present Market Square the Conduit ceased to occupy the central position it had held in the former L-shaped market area, and in 1855, after 240 years of useful service, it was removed to its present position at Brookside, and an inscription was added recording its history.

Interesting relics of early Cambridge town life are the massive foundations and fragments of stout walls seen in the recently demolished (1915) building adjoining the Guildhall, the confiscated house of Benjamin the Jew, given to the town in 1224 by Henry III. for the purposes of a prison. When, in 1790, the old Gaol was removed to a new site at the rear of the Spinning House, this ancient building was converted into a public house known as the Town Arms.

Another link with the past is the Three Tuns, where, Pepys tells us, he " drank pretty hard and many healths to the King, etc., till it began to be darkish." On the cistern-head of the rainpipe may be seen embossed, three tuns and the date 1727.

Erected in the newly-built room for the Borough Librarian is one of several fine old clunch fireplaces found some years since in John Vesey's house, once standing at the corner of Petty Cury, on the site now occupied by Messrs. Hallack and Bond's premises. Interesting pictures of the old Market-place may be seen on the walls of the Public Reading Room; one, a print of Rowlandson's, showing the Hill in 1801; another being a water-colour sketch of Pump Lane with the old shops of Johnson the grocer, and Sharman the toy-dealer.   There is also a small view of Hobson's Conduit and the Town Hall.   In Cooper's *Memorials* will be found an excellent view of the Hill by Le Keux; while the *Cambridge Portfolio* gives us a detailed drawing of the Conduit.

The following interesting extract from the Bowtell MSS. preserved in the library of Downing College may appropriately conclude our account of the Market Place as it existed in olden times :

As late as the reign of George II. very few tradesmen's shops were furnished with glazed windows.   It was not until about the year 1700 that sash windows were first introduced in Cambridge, and then only partially in the fronts of principal mansions . . .   The first entire front of a house in Cambridge improved by sash windows was on the E. side of the Market Hill, A.D. 1741, then occupied by Mr Ald. White, and now (1812) by Mr Orridge, a druggist. During a space of almost 30 years subsequent to that period most of the shops even in the principal streets continued to yield but a mean appearance.   Their window-shutters were similar to those of tradesmen's booths in Stourbridge Fair, formed bivalvular, having two hatches movable on hinges ; thereby for the admission of light, the lowermost was let down and supported in a horizontal position, either by means of folding joints, or by resting on grotesque posts for the exhibition of goods thereon.   The other half was held up by iron hooks fastened under the eaves of Penthouses, which are annexed to the lower story of almost every tenement, and served to protect the vendable articles from damages which they might otherwise have sustained from stormy weather.

It was at half-past twelve on the night of Saturday, 15 September 1849, that the alarm of fire was raised at a clothier's shop kept by a man named Lodge, which occupied approximately the position now taken up by the bookstall of our friend Mr David. The fire-engines of the police, the various Insurance Offices, and those belonging to Trinity and St John's were soon upon the spot, but alas ! the keys of Hobson's Conduit could not be found.   The final discovery of the keys only increased the prevailing excitement and confusion, for the firemen were soon vigorously squabbling over the limited water supply of the Conduit.   Matters were improved, however, by the numberless buckets and pails which were literally showered upon the crowds of willing helpers, who soon formed themselves into lines of supply to the ten engines now upon the scene ; some of these lines extended down Garret Hostel Lane as far as the river, and all the pumps in the vicinity contributed their share.

Meanwhile the fire raged furiously, and all efforts to subdue it were of little avail. Just as St Mary's clock struck two the walls of Lodge's house fell with a tremendous crash, sending up such a terrific cloud of dust, smoke, and embers that for a few moments it completely obscured the flames. The fire was now a veritable furnace, and from its origin at Lodge's extended along Market Hill through Kent's house to the premises of Pearless, the draper, where a thick partition wall arrested its advance in this direction. On the opposite side it spread from the corner house of Orridge the chemist to that of Milligan, the tailor, in St Mary's Street, and was soon devouring the oil and colour stores of Messrs. Moden next door.

The demolition, at about three o'clock, of another corner house beyond, owned by James Wonfor, was of little avail, for the flames spread behind into Warwick Street, and only when they had reached and destroyed an unoccupied house next to the King's Head public house were they finally checked by the tremendous and gallant efforts of a band of builder's workmen some three hours later. Many people now feared greatly for the safety of the premises on the north side of St Mary's Street, viz. those of Messrs. Peters, Purvis, and Bacon, but by a thorough drenching of the walls with water they were happily saved. It is interesting to note that as an additional precaution, sodden blankets were placed upon the roofs and others hung from the front windows ; it is clear that there was very real cause for anxiety, since Peters the silversmith had all the more valuable portion of the stock removed to the bakehouse of Emmerson in Warwick Street, which it will be remembered backed on to the chancel wall of St Mary's Church.

Meantime, throughout the night, scenes of wild confusion occurred amongst the panic-stricken crowd in their efforts to save all that was possible from the fire. Furniture from the threatened or burning houses was hastily removed, and the lighter pieces hurled by their distracted owners into the street below. People in their frenzy threw crockery out of the window, and carefully carried hardware out of the front door ; whilst at Messrs Moden's, the colourmen, pickles were poured into oil, mustard was emptied into greasy casks ; the most heterogeneous articles were crushed together in every available box and case, and the whole ruined mass was thrown into two carts which had been brought up to assist in the salvage ! Then a sudden diversion took place in the form of an unrehearsed display of fireworks at the chemist's at the corner.

In the midst of Orridge's blazing shop was a jet of gas, clearly distinguishable from the livid and deeper shade of the flames springing from burning timber and other materials. The changing colours of the flame, as first one chemical and then another acted upon it, were of an almost incredible beauty and as varied as the hues of the rainbow. This escape of gas continued for some time before the true cause of the flame was discovered, when messengers were sent off post-haste to the Gasworks to get it turned off at the mains, as it was feared that serious explosions might occur. All this time there was great fear and anxiety as no one could tell in which direction the walls were liable to fall, when suddenly the church clock struck half-past three and, again by a singular coincidence, as though accepting the signal, the whole house instantly collapsed with a terrific crash, sending up a shower of bricks and burning embers to a great distance.

By six o'clock on the following (Sunday) morning all immediate loss of property was at an end. Eight houses had been totally destroyed, reckoning from and including Pearless's on the Market Hill, down St Mary's Street, and round the corner of Warwick Street to the King's Head, while the neighbouring houses were much damaged by fire and water. All through Sunday several of the engines continued to play upon the ruins, to prevent any possibility of the fire spreading to the remaining houses.

As evidence of the high wind that was blowing during the fire, charred leaves from a Bible and one of Pearless's invoices were picked up at Castle End, close to the Shirehall.

Both the Senate Hill and the southern side of Market Hill were made the dumping ground for the motley collection of household goods, stores, and broken furniture snatched from the flames, and this was given over to the protection of the police, who had a busy time restoring the numberless articles to their proper owners and warning off suspicious characters attracted to the scene.

The police, under Inspector Jaggard, together with the special constables, under the superintendence of the Mayor (Alderman Finch) and several magistrates, received high commendation for preserving order and preventing depredation ; Alderman Brown particularly came under notice for his strenuous and active efforts in assisting wherever help was most needed, and among other ready workers were Dr Paget, Dr Bumpstead, Mr Crowfoot, of Caius, Mr Ficklin, and other well-known citizens.

During the progress of the fire, curiosity and excitement were aroused by the sound of the Crier's bell, which Isaac Moule (the Crier) was vigorously ringing, whilst publishing lustily on all parts of the Hill the loss of a gold watch by a person in the crowd : another loss was, however, beyond the aid of the Crier's " Oyez," viz. a pair of Cromwell's boots, reputed to be of undoubted authenticity, which were consumed in the ruins of Orridge's house. The high hats then worn by the police afforded many times a mark for the facetious young man in charge of the Phoenix engine, who scored several direct hits with the water-jet, much to the merriment of the onlookers.

In the confusion arising from the hurried flight of families from the danger zone in Pump-lane, George Andrews, who eventually succeeded Moule as Town Crier, and was the father of a numerous progeny, while congratulating himself on having got them all away safely, had the good sense to count them, when to his horror he found that one of his brood was missing ! A hurried return, however, to the house and a careful survey of the beds, revealed his little one deep in slumber under its coverlet !

News of the alarming extent of the fire rapidly reached the neighbouring villages, and drew large crowds to the Market Place as Sunday wore on ; towards evening much anxiety was caused by fear that the fire of the still burning cellars might extend to the adjoining houses ; this, however, was soon allayed by the watchful

firemen. The reassured onlookers now slowly wandered homewards, to recoup in sleep what they had lost in their unbroken vigil
of the previous night.   Though there were many narrow escapes
from falling walls and timber, no loss of life or limb is recorded, but
its devastating and far-reaching results will for long retain a place
in our local annals.

Opinion as to the origin of the fire appears to have been almost
unanimous and freely expressed, with the result that several of the
more outspoken citizens were the unhappy recipients on the Monday
morning of writs for *scandalum magnatum* issued at the instance of
Lodge, upon whose premises the fire originated.   The serious nature,
however, of the generally accepted opinion impelled the Coroner to
exercise his power of convening an inquest to inquire into the origin
of the outbreak, and a jury was summoned for the same evening at
the Town Hall.   As this was the first occasion in Cambridge history
of an inquest of such a nature, no little excitement was aroused ;
the prolonged and searching examination of the many witnesses
necessitated an adjournment till the following evening (Tuesday),
resulting then in an open verdict.

To describe the various Committees, Vestry Meetings, Commissions, and Boards, with the usual accompaniment of arguments,
bickerings, dissensions, negotiations, and what not, which arose
in consequence of the fire, would be wearisome to my readers.
Suffice it to say that the Town Council acted with energy and the
Board of Improvement Commissioners, with Dr Thackeray as
Chairman, undertook to deal with the Market Place site.   Disagree-
ment as to whether St Mary's Passage should be opened to vehicular
traffic or remain a footpath caused some delay, but in the following
year was passed the Cambridge Corporation Act of 1850, which gave
full powers to the authorities, who, in due course, completed the
work begun by the fire, and evolved the fine Market Square as known
to us to-day.

For the dual origin of Cambridge and evidence of yet another
Market Place and Cross at Castle End, we must refer the reader to
the important paper[1] by the Master of Jesus upon the fascinating
period of Cambridge history during the Heptarchy.

[1] " The Dual Origin of the Town of Cambridge," by Arthur Gray : *C.A.S.*, 4to
publ., N.S., No. 1, 1908.

CHAPTER VII.

The Cambridge Loyal Association [of Volunteers], 1797

HE part played by Cambridgeshire in our military history may very properly be regarded by its inhabitants with pride. When the invading Danes landed at Ipswich in the year 1010, and put the East Angles to flight " then stood Grantabric shire fastly against them "— so runs the Anglo-Saxon Chronicle.

As an important member of the Eastern Counties Association formed for providing recruits for the Parliamentary Army, Cambridge had her share in the Great Civil War[1] and in the recent Great European War the Cambridgeshire Regiment won enduring fame.

When, again, a volunteer movement arose in response to Napoleon's threatened invasion of Britain, Cambridge, as we shall see, entered with enthusiasm into the scheme.

Cooper's Annals and the early files of the *Cambridge Chronicle* give much curious information on this subject. The copious manuscript notes of John Bowtell attached to a copy of the *Rules and Orders of the Cambridge Loyal Association* in the University Library may conveniently be consulted in my Memoir of that Worthy in Vol. XI. of the Camb. Antiquarian Society's Proceedings, whilst the late Mr J. E. Foster's paper (in the same volume) *On a badge of the Cambridge Volunteers of* 1798 contains further interesting facts.

From these authorities we learn that during 1798 no less a sum than £11,000 was subscribed by the University and Town towards a

---

[1] Alfred Kingston, *East Anglia and the Great Civil War,* 1902.

115

general contribution for the defence of the country, and two military Associations existed in the Borough, one called The Patriotic Association of Cambridge Volunteers, and the other The Cambridge Loyal Association. The latter was formed at a meeting held at the Town Hall, over which Mr John Mortlock, then Mayor, presided ; whilst the *Cambridge Chronicle* of 26 May 1798, gives an account of an inspection of the first-named body, and a paragraph

REVERSE AND OBVERSE OF VOLUNTEER BADGE.

in the issue for 23 June refers to the burial of George Favell, Corporal in the Loyal Association, which the members attended.

Bowtell gives a list of the members of the Loyal Association (formed 24 February 1797) which, in addition to the name of John Nicholson, the son of the more celebrated " Maps," includes the names of many of our old Cambridge families, such as Hallack, Palmer, Leach, Hattersley, and Sussum. On 11 April 1797, " An Order was made for mustering on Parker's Piece instead of Sidney College Close."

In April of the following year " a proposal was made by the Committee for the Corps to offer their services to the Government to serve in any part of Great Britain in case of invasion by a foreign enemy, which was daily expected," whilst another proposal bound them " during the war to escort any prisoners . . . baggage, etc., which might be brought into this town to any place required, and to mount guard over any prisoners of war confined in this Town of Cambridge." October brought with it a change of training ground ; Parker's Piece was forsaken, and it was resolved that " The Corps should meet in the Market Place on the first Monday in every month, at nine o'clock in the morning, for the purpose of military exercise." Meanwhile another important matter had not been neglected, the matter of a uniform worthy of the gallant spirit of its wearers. It consisted of a " Blue coat lined and turned up with white shalloon, plain yellow buttons, scarlet collar and cuffs, white pantaloons, half-gaiters of black cloth with black buttons," the whole surmounted by a " Round hat with bearskin, black cockade and a black feather."

ALDERMAN BURLEIGH, from a painting in the Cambridge Free Library.

Our Market Place has witnessed many exciting scenes, but surely nothing finer than the spectacle of this trusty band engaged in "military exercise " on certain frosty mornings in the winter of 1798, when George the Third was king. How clattered the arms of that martial array ! What a proud

Rec^d of Dr Davy the sum of thirteen pounds
for cartredges for the use of the university Drile L^o
April 1. 1803   Willm Gallyon
£ 13. 0. 0

Dr Davy. Vicechancellor for the use of the
University Drill

1803   to W Gallyon

Nov 22   200 Cartredges at ? per ?   0 = 12 = 0
     25   800 Cartredges   2 = 8 = 0
     28   1560 Cartredges   4 = 13 = ?
          700 Ball cartredges   3 = 10 = 0
          1660 Cartredges   4 = 19 = ?
     9/   2200 Cartredges   6 = 12 = 0
           13 Stan of arms at 2.12.6 each   47 = 5 = 0
           13 Set of accoutrements 1.12.0   28 = 16 = 0
          Numbering arms & ?   0 = 10 = 8
                                                     £ 99 = 6 = 2
          deducted for cartredges   22 = 15 = ?
          1804,   76 = 11 = ?
     16 Aug^t
          rec^d the above of Dr Davy
                    By Wm Gallyon

RECEIPTS FOR THE FIRST WEAPONS, ACCOUTREMENTS, AND AMMUNITION,
supplied to the University Volunteers of 1804.

assembly of sweethearts and mothers ! How the populace cheered, and what sad havoc was wrought by bearskin and plume among the hearts of the fair members of the admiring crowd !

> Ah me ! my retrospective soul !
> As over memory's muster-roll
>   I cast my eyes anew,
> Our ghostly fathers all the while
> Rise up before me, rank and file,
>   And form in dim review.[1]

On one occasion this patriotic corps came in touch with a live enemy. Bowtell records that :

One Frenchman who had been a midshipman in the enemies' service, and who had escaped from his imprisonment at Yaxley barracks on the 4th of June, 1798, was taken by a party of this corps and escorted again from Cambridge to the said barracks (eight and twenty miles) at the charge of £6 0s. 6d., which was freely paid by the members of this Loyal Association.

It is with no small satisfaction that we learn :

As an acknowledgment of the voluntary readiness in which this corps held themselves to serve their country, the sum of £200 was voted to them by the town and county of Cambridge for their use accordingly.

The loyal efforts of the people of Cambridge appeared to be no longer required when the peace of Amiens was declared in 1802. But we were again at war with France in 1803, and Cambridge rose to the occasion with renewed and refreshing vigour. A further sum of £2,100, says Mr Foster, was raised for military purposes, again a meeting was held under the presidency of the Mayor, Mr John Cheetham Mortlock, and a new corps of Volunteers, consisting largely of members of the two bodies referred to above, came into being with the Mayor himself as Lieut.-Colonel.

The corps began with 450 men, organised in six companies, and two more were added, contributed respectively by Bassingbourn and Chesterton. Mr Cooper gives a list of the officers down to 1808, amongst whom many well-known Cambridge names occur, beside that of the Colonel, such as John Deighton, father of the late Mr Deighton, the surgeon ; Elliot Smith, the celebrated auctioneer and land agent of Cambridge, and father of Mr John Smith, late of 1, Brookside ;

[1] Adapted from T. Hood.

Richard Foster, father of Miss Sophia Foster, late of 17, Bateman Street ; Henry Balls, father of the late Mr Charles Balls ; David Bradwell, father of the late Mr Thomas Bradwell, the builder and Robert Bevan Turner, father of the late Mr Turner, the post master, and grandfather of Mr George Turner, Mayor in 1915-6.

ROBERT TURNER in the uniform of the
old Patriotic Volunteers.

Other local corps were established at this time, and amongst those who took a prominent part in this growing volunteer movement is the name of Barnet Beales, great-grandfather of the present Lieut.-Col. Beales, who formerly commanded the Headquarters Companies of the Cambridgeshire Territorial Regiment.

At the Public Record Office are the pay sheets of the Cambridge and Cambridgeshire Riflemen, organised in 1804 under the command of Mr Charles Humfrey. In 1806 a second company was established, commanded by Mr Arthur Deck. Soon county companies began to be established—but the interested reader must gather the rest of the story from Mr Foster's pages.

A UNIVERSITY VOLUNTEER OF 1804, reproduced from Harraden's *Costume of the ... University of Cambridge*, 1803-05.

Ob. An
Ch. 1645.

Ætatis
suæ 96.

A Grave Divine; precise, not turbulent;
And never guilty of the Churches rent:
Meek even to sinners; most devout to GOD:
This is but part of the due praise of DOD.

C. B.

THE REV. JOHN DOD, from a portrait by Cross reproduced from
Tracts . . . relating to Northamptonshire, 2nd Ser. No. 4, 1881.

CHAPTER VIII.

A Little Sermon upon Malt

T HE following impromptu Sermon upon " Malt," as applicable to-day as at the time when it was delivered, seems worthy of preservation.

Its author, the Rev. Dr Dod (1549-1645), who is said to have preached it under the peculiar circumstances narrated below, was a Fellow of Jesus College. A pronounced Puritan, though a staunch Royalist, he was in the habit, while a resident at Cambridge, of riding out weekly to Ely to preach, and it is probable that it was on one of these excursions that this remarkable address was given to his ribald audience.

" Old Mr Dod," as he was affectionately called by his contemporaries, was a great character and wit. His published "Sayings" were widely read, and it is from a copy of these in the form of a broadside, now very scarce, that we have selected the following from among Dr Dod's many popular proverbs :

Four Things we may learn from Children ; 1. They take no unnecessary Care. 2. They sleep without Malice. 3. They are content with their Condition. 4. They are humble ; the Child of a King, will play with the Child of a Beggar.

The Sinner is the Devil's Miller, always grinding, and the Devil is always filling the hopper, that the Mill may not stand still.

Brown Bread with the Gospel is good Fare.

Many versions of his quaint Sermon have appeared from time to time. The one we have selected is taken from a tract first published in 1777. There also exist three copies of the Sermon in MS., two being in the British Museum, *Sloane MSS.*, the other in the

Bodleian Library, *Ashmolean MSS.* The texts of these, together with the printed pamphlet of 1777 are given in a volume entitled *Tracts . . . relating to the County of Northampton*, 2nd Ser., No. IV. (1881), with a preface by John Taylor, where, referring to the MSS., he tells us that " the dates of the MSS. of the three texts are all contemporary with Dod.   That of the text found in the Bodleian Library is written by Ashmole himself on the back of a letter signed " J. Suckling, 1629."

A

S E R M O N

upon the word

MALT

———

Mr Dod being for some time in a village near Cambridge, and having frequently observed the irregular behaviour of *some* of the *students* of the University, particularly excess in drinking, to which they were *greatly* addicted, took occasion to explode such practices in public from the pulpit.

" It happened some time after this, several of these young sparks riding out, met Mr DOD on the road, they espied him some distance off, and *immediately* on first sight of him, cried out, Here comes father DOD !   Now we'll have some sport with the old man."   According they consulted each other, and *soon* resolved in what manner they would divert themselves on this occasion, namely, by *compelling* him to preach them a Sermon in the stump of a hollow *tree*, that happened to be on the spot.   Mr DOD kept jogging on, little thinking of any *plot* forming against him, at length arrived where the *students* were waiting for *him*.   The *compliments* at this *meeting* having passed, they enquired of the good *man* if the *report* they had heard of his having preached against *drunkenness* of late, was true ; Mr DOD replied, that perceiving the *prevalency* of such *evils*, and *especially* amongst those from whom *better* things might be expected, he *could not* dispense with a delay in *reproving* the same, *consistant with his public character as a Minister ;* therefore he had inveighed against *a vice so very detestable in the sight of GOD and all good men.*

The *collegians* then said they had a favour to request of him that he would *indulge* them with a Sermon from a *text* of *their own chusing*.   To this Mr DOD replied in the *negative*, alledging it was *highly* unreasonable to *require* a man, *publicly* to deliver his sentiments, upon any subject, without *first* giving him an *opportunity* to ruminate the same in his own thoughts in *private* ; besides, adds he, I am upon a journey, in pursuit of other concerns at present, therefore desire you will lay aside, and desist from any further solicitations in this affair.

To which the students answered " they were thoroughly persuaded he was master of elocution, *never* at a loss for matter upon *any* subject, that they could not *bear* the thoughts of a denial, and perhaps such a *fair* opportunity might never again present itself."

Mr DOD seeing himself thus beset, replied : " Well, gentlemen, as you are thus *urgent* for my compliance, pray what is the *subject* I am to handle." They answered, " Sir, the word—MALT ;—and, for want of a better, here, Sir, is your pulpit " ; pointing to the stump of a hollow *tree* at hand.

Hereupon, the *venerable man* mounted the rostrum, and addressed his hearers in the following manner :

Beloved,

I am a little man, come at a short warning,—to deliver a brief discourse— upon a small subject,—to a thin congregation,—and from an unworthy pulpit.

Beloved, my text is
MALT
which cannot be divided into words, it being but one ; nor into syllables, it being but one ; therefore, of necessity, I must reduce it into letters, which I find to be these :

M.—A.—L.—T.

M — my beloved, is Moral.
A — is Allegorical.
L — is Litteral.
AND
T — is Theological.

The moral is set forth to teach you drunkards good manners ; therefore

M — my Masters
A — All of you
L — Listen
T — to my Text

The allegorical is when one thing is spoken, and another is intended ; the thing expressed is MALT ; the thing signified is the oil of MALT, which you Bacchanals make

M — your Meat,
A — your Apparel,
L — your Liberty,
AND
T — your Text.

The litteral is according to the letter

M — Much
A — Ale,
L — Little
T — Thrift.

The theological is according to the effects it produces, which I find to consist of two kinds.

THE
First, Respects this life.
THE
Second, That which is to come.

The effects it produces in this world, are in some,

M — Murder,
            in others,
A — Adultery,
            in all,
L — Licentious Lives,
            in many
T — Treason.

The effects consequent in the world to come, are,

M — Misery
A — Anguish
L — Lamentation
T — Torment.

Thus, Sirs, having briefly opened and explained my *short* text, give me leave to make a little use and improvement of the foregoing

AND
First, by way of exhortation,

M — my Masters
A — All of you
L — Leave off
T — Tippling.

OR,
Secondly, by way of commination,

M — my Masters
A — All of you
L — Look for
T — Torment.

Now to wind up the whole and draw to a close take with you the characteristic of a drunkard.

A drunkard is the annoyance of modesty.
The spoil of civility.
His own shame.
His wife's sorrow.
His children's curse.
His neighbour's scoff.
The alehouse man's benefactor.
The devil's drudge.
A *walking* swill bowl.
The picture of a beast.
And, monster of a man.

DITTON CHURCH from the Towing Path.

CHAPTER IX.

The Fen Ditton Penance of 1849

IN the comfortable times of Queen Victoria, which now seem dim and almost mythical, the pretty village of Fen Ditton, familiar to us in race-week, with the gay and happy throng of June visitors crowding its meadows and river-bank, was, on the morning of Sunday, 6 May 1849, the scene of a disgraceful brawl, arising through the remarkable announcement that one of the villagers was sentenced by the Court of Arches to make public penance in the parish church at the morning service.

The penitent was the local fiddler, one Edward Smith, a gardener and former parish sexton, who two years previously, at a public house in the village, when half drunk and half foolish, had made libellous imputations upon the character of the rector's wife. The aggrieved lady, as soon as this reached her ears, lost no time in promoting a suit in the Ecclesiastical Court, whence, after two years of the law's delay, it reached the Court of Arches, with the result that the defendant Smith was, in addition to his sentence of penance, condemned in costs amounting to £42 17s. 6d.

From the period of the passing of the sentence the gossips of the county had talked of nothing else ; and Smith's offence was soon forgotten amid curiosity to see a man standing in church in a white sheet (as it was seriously reported would be the case) and to observe his conduct in such a singular situation.

On the Sunday appointed nearly all roads and lanes leading to this picturesque village church were thronged at an early hour by a motley crowd, whose boisterous behaviour was strangely out of keeping with the peaceful countryside, bathed in the sunshine of early spring. These unwelcome invaders congregated in the church-yard on their arrival, and it was computed that before the bells had done ringing there were not less than 3,000 strangers in the village. This huge mob, though largely made up of the élite of Barnwell, included also, it must be confessed, many of the more respectable inhabitants of Cambridge and the county, some of the latter, indeed, having previously applied for reserved pews so that they could witness the novel and eagerly looked for performance and the un-willing actor who was to appear in the leading part. These, however, with most of the regular attendants at the church, soon retired when they saw the assemblage of low characters that had gathered together, evidently intent on mischief.

Around and within the church porch so dense was the crowd that for some time the clerk was unable even to reach the doors, and when at last he succeeded in his efforts, and had unlocked and thrown them open, a rush took place that would have disgraced the gallery of a London theatre on Boxing Night, and every available spot was occupied in less than five minutes.

The chancel-screen was half hidden by bargees sitting astride it ; the capitals of the pillars had each its human occupant ; and the building, which is said to be capable of seating 1,000 persons, was crowded to suffocation, the majority of the audience standing upon the seats and eagerly fighting for places which would command the best view of the expected penitent.

No sooner was the body of the church filled than large numbers made their way in by clambering along the eaves, entering by the upper windows, and standing upon the top of the wainscoting. This ruffianly mode of entrance involved the smashing of much glass, and the excitement due to fragments falling upon the crowd below aroused a vast amount of coarse mirth.

Meanwhile, at the rectory, close by, another scene was being enacted which, though less boisterous than that just described, was doubtless conducted with no small amount of asperity and warmth. The rector, now fully alive to the threatening attitude of the crowd outside, and anxious to irritate no further the hornet's nest that had been roused, earnestly implored his wife to abandon the proceedings and absolve Smith from his penance. But he had not reckoned on the fury of a woman scorned ! The lady, who appears to have been as wilful as her elderly husband was weak, remained deaf to all entreaty, gave a positive refusal, and insisted on the ceremony being carried out.

Accordingly, on the stroke of eleven, there issued from the rectory in solemn procession to the church the Rev. A. H. Small, of Emmanuel College, who had undertaken to do duty on the occasion, followed by the plaintiff and Mr C. H. Cooper (the antiquary), of Cambridge, and the lady's attorney, and, finally, by the rector himself. " When an old bachelor marries a young wife," bitterly reflects Sir Peter Teazle, " what is he to expect ? " Similar thoughts must have passed through the unhappy rector's mind as his wife swept before him into the rectory pew, and the audience paused for a moment to stare at the little party and then settled down to enjoy the fun.

No sooner had Mr Small pronounced the opening sentences of the service than he was saluted by shouts of " Speak up, old boy," followed by a chorus of laughter, which was frequently repeated as some adventurous wight failed in his attempt to scramble up a pillar into a more commanding position. So frequent and so ribald were the interruptions that Mr Small, after reading the lesson, stopped, amidst derisive jeers, on his way from the reading-desk to take counsel with the rector, who prudently advised the omission of the hymns.

By this time, however, the jostling congregation had flooded the chancel and even occupied the altar table itself, compelling the unfortunate minister to take refuge in the pulpit, where, having hastily concluded the service, he proceeded to preach from the text, singularly inappropriate under the circumstances, " Judge not, that ye be not judged."

The audience, which at first had been good-humoured, had now become impatient. The sermon was frequently interrupted by shouts of " 'Ere's Smith," contradicted by cries of " No, that ain't 'im," " That's 'im up there " (in the pulpit). With commendable patience the preacher endeavoured to continue his discourse until his voice was finally drowned by cat-calls, whistles, laughter, and crashing of breaking glass, culminating in the pandemonium caused by a dog fight promoted by the rabble in the churchyard. The interest aroused by this gave way, in its turn, to that excited by a cry of " Smith is coming," several times reiterated ; and the struggle that ensued for places commanding a view of the aisle up which he was to proceed to his appointed position opposite the reading desk baffles all description.

At last his coming was announced by a shout from the crowd outside that shook the building. The preacher had no sooner left the pulpit than it was occupied by a band of ruffians, who maintained their position throughout. The shouting outside subsided as Smith entered the church, but was immediately taken up by its occupants, who gave three lusty cheers, followed by clapping of hands, whoops, yells and other discordant sounds.

When the penitent reached the reading-desk the crush was so great that he had to be lifted into the pew of one of the church-wardens, where he was mounted on a hassock placed on a seat immediately facing the pew of the much embarrassed rector and his now terror-stricken wife. Nothing but this arrangement would satisfy the audience, for those were the days of enclosed high pews, and the culprit would otherwise have been unseen by the majority. Meanwhile quiet was in some degree restored by Smith, who waved above his head the paper from which he was to read his recantation. Mr Small repeatedly attempted to speak, but was constantly met by loud cries of " Smith, Smith, one cheer more for Smith," and by Smith as often calling lustily, " Silence for the minister." The uproar continuing, the penitent, who seems to have borne himself well under the circumstances, beckoned to one of the churchwardens in the same pew with him, and asked what was to be done, saying, " You see what a state the church is in ; you know what is best ; I am your prisoner, and will do as you think proper." While he was making these observations, a broom found in a corner of the church was thrown across it and fell within a yard of the pulpit. Then came a hassock—then another ; and finally the pews were torn up, broken into pieces, and thrown in all directions.

While the penitent was endeavouring to read his recantation, the hassocks came as thick as hail, and the bursting of one was the signal for the most uproarious laughter, as the chaff scattered on the heads of those below. Short pipes were now unblushingly brought out, their smoke filling the church, but the climax was reached when several people seized the bell ropes and caused a violent jangling of the bells, completely drowned, however, by the din raging below !

At the conclusion of Smith's recantation, Mr Small hurriedly left the building in disgust, but not until he had been struck by a hassock. Smith at the same moment moved out of the pew to leave the church also. On reaching the floor he was taken up by the mob amid shouts of " Bravo, Smith : well done, Smith," and finally carried out on men's shoulders amidst hearty cheers.

On his way to the Plough Inn he was called upon to make a speech, and in reply said to the immense crowd that was around him, " I am sorry I cannot ask you all to dinner, for I am but a poor man." During his enforced but triumphant procession through the village, the inhabitants rushed out to shake hands with him, women threw up their bonnets, and men and children shouted. On his entering the Plough the house was immediately filled with his admirers, who, as might have been expected, spent the remainder of the afternoon in smoking and drinking on the green. Smith, however, with good taste, retired to his home, saying that he wished there to be no further disturbance. The rector and his wife, on the other hand, not without good reason, were hooted on their exit from the church, and afterwards followed to the rectory by a howling mob, who did not disperse until they had stoned and smashed every window in the house.

Thus ended a penance in which the faults of the accused sink into insignificance before those of the accusers, but for whose incredible folly and gross mismanagement the scenes we have just described would never have taken place.

Throughout the day a collection was being made through the village by men with boxes, May-Day fashion, the supplication being " Please to remember Smith." The sum collected was considerable, and it is stated that the amount required for the discharge of the defendant's liabilities in the suit was exceeded, several of the farmers in the neighbourhood having previously sent in subscriptions ; but it is to be feared that the greater part of the proceeds was the same day spent at the Plough, as July found Smith a prisoner for non-payment of the costs in the county gaol, where he lay for five months pending his discharge at the Insolvent Debtors' Court.

A friend who remembers the penitent has supplied the following information :

I knew old Ted Smith well. If you gave him sixpence, he would tell you the story. He was a great character, and kept a Commonplace Book, in which he put down various incidents interlarded with other matters, such as a good cure for the stomach-ache, etc. He was a gardener at the rectory when the discovery was made by him, which led to his talking too freely in the public-house, and to old Henry Muggleton, the carpenter and parish constable, having to make further searches in the pond that at that time existed in the paddock, but was later filled up when the river was dredged. [We refrain from entering into the groundless rumours, prevalent at the time, which led to these "searches" and alleged " discoveries."] Ted Smith's book I could never get hold of after his death, as it went to America in possession of a man named Pampling. In the mob in the church at the penance were many undergraduates. . . . Smith was to have read his recantation in a white sheet. But he declared that if they compelled him to do so, he would blacken his face. As there was nothing illegal in this, and he could not be prevented from doing it, he was relieved from the necessity of wearing the sheet.

In striking contrast to the foregoing fiasco, resulting from a foolish attempt to revive ecclesiastical punishment long since out of date, is the record of a certain fair, but frail penitent of the same village, who, many generations before in the same church, dutifully and humbly made her penance as directed by Holy Church :

Sexto die mensis Januarii, anno 1593. Parte of pennance injoyned unto Agnes Black, of Fen Ditton. The saied penitent shall uppon Sundaie, beinge the eighte daie of February next cominge, clothed in a white sheete downe to the grounde and havinge a white wande in her hande, resorte unto the parish churche-porche of Fen Ditton aforesaied, and there shall stande from the seconde peele to morninge prayers untill the readinge of the seconde lesson, desiringe the people that passe into the churche to praie to God for her, and to forgive her ; at which time the minister there shall come down to this penitent and fetch her into the churche, readinge the psalm of Miserere in Englishe, and place her in the middle alley a-parte from all other people, where she shall penitently kneel untill the readings of the ten commandments, at which time the minister there shall come to this penitent and cause her to saie and confesse as followethe, viz., " Good people, I acknowledge and confesse, that I have offended Almightie God . . ." etc.   And if the penitent doing this uppon all the saied three severall Sundaies or holy daies, she shall under the handes of the minister and churchwardens there personallie certifie togeather with those present the xxvii daie of February at Greate St Marie's Churche in Cambridge, and then and there receave such further order herein as shall be appointed.

The due fulfilment of the above injunction is shown by the following certificate :

𝕿𝖍𝖎𝖘 penitent had done hir penance three severall Sundaies or holy daies in the parish churche of Fen Ditton according to the premises.

Ita est ut testatur, Thomas Goobed, cur, ibid churche.

The Five Miles from Anywhere.

In the Fens

CHAPTER X.

The Upware Republic

IN the Autumn of 1917, shortly after the publication of the first three *Walks* in the *Cambridge Chronicle*, I received from the Editor a small packet which had been left at his office addressed to me. The unfamiliar handwriting aroused a mild curiosity which was not lessened upon finding that the packet contained a letter and a little weather-beaten note-book.

The writer, a native of Cambridge, though personally unknown to me, stated that he had secured the volume for a few pence at a London book-barrow and, after kindly saying with what interest he had read my *Walks*, requested my acceptance of his find, of which I was to make whatever use I liked. Eagerly opening the book, I read upon its fly-leaf " Upware Republic Society, 1851," and a brief examination of its pages sufficed to show that I was the fortunate possessor of the records of a long-forgotten club of under-graduates who were in the habit of coming to the lonely Inn in the Fens called The Five Miles from Anywhere, in order to enjoy a few hours' escape from the restraints of academic life.

The title-page runs as follows :

UPWARE, NOV. 1851.

VISITORS' BOOK

***

Members of the Upware Republic Society are
particularly requested to enter their names with
date before leaving "Five Miles from Anywhere."

***

BY ORDER OF

CONSULS { J. WOLSTENHOLME, Joh.
{ J. JENNINGS, Trin.

VICE-CONSUL THOS. APPLEBY.

Ordered by the Consuls and the other Officers that if the
names of any visitors are not put down at the time of the visit the
same shall be entered as soon after as possible by any officer
staying at Upware.

No rules appear, and the constitution of the Society can only be surmised from the following official titles that occur, namely : Consul, President, State Chaplain, Minister of Education, Professor, Interpreter, Champion, Tapster, Treasurer, and Secretary. Appleby, the landlord of the Inn, was dubbed Vice-Consul. Assisted by his wife, he attended to the creature comforts of visitors, and appears to have acquired no little fame for " egg-flip," one of the mulled drinks then much in fashion.

The Club Book records the visits of no less than three hundred members and visitors to its headquarters, and of many recurring signatures those of the two Consuls, J. Wolstenholme (St John's College) and F. T. Jennings (Trinity) together with that of the " Champion," W. S. Harrison (Trinity) appear most frequently.

As might be expected, few of this large body of signatories made sufficient mark in the world to render them traceable in later days. There remains, however, an interesting residue of men who achieved distinction, and I now proceed to note some of the more important names :

JOSEPH WOLSTENHOLME (1829-1891).
    St John's ; M.A. 1853, Sc.D. 1883 ; graduated as 3rd Wrangler 1850, elected Fellow 1852 ; Fellow of Christ's 1852-69 ; Math. Prof. of the Royal Engineer. College, Cooper's Hill 1871-89. Author of numerous mathematical work.
    Wolstenholme was one of the first two Consuls of the " Upware Republic " to be elected. In 1853 he signed the Visitors' Book as ex-consul, and in 1854 we find the dignified signature of Joseph Burwelliensis State Chaplain. The following year " After an official visit to Burwell feast," made in company with Consul Sin Clarke and President Hartley, he signs yet more grandiloquently as " Josephus Burwelliensis Archiepiscopus."

EDMUND GEORGE HARVEY (1828-1884).
    Queens' ; B.A. 1850, Rector of St Mary's, Truro, 1860. Vicar of Mullyon, 1865. Musical composer and author. Composed Gregorian chants, hymn tunes, etc.
    In a retrospective note in the Club book, dated 1 Jan. 1854, Harvey describes himself as : " The quondam Count of Upware and Beach who held sway over these parts previous to the establishment of a Kingdom and after that the Republic ; after an absence of several years (having during the past summer taken a crew thro' France and Germany in a pair-oar) pulled down to this most lovely of all parts of the earth on 26 Dec. 1851

and was with his friend much rejoiced to find (although his former powerful dominion is not mentioned, nor that of his illustrious predecessor) that the affairs of the Republic are in so prosperous a condition.

The name of the 1st Prince is already too well known to be now mentioned tho' it is an unaccountable omission on the part of this Republic. Again was it not the Count who inscribed " the Pewter " and the walls of the house, was it not the Emperor who first conquered the prejudice of society and invaded these parts ?   Therefore, though their absolute sway is now past and gone, let not their names be forgotten by the present and future members of the Republic."

JOHN ELDON GORST (1835-1916).
St John's ; M.A. 1860 ; knighted 1885 ; Solicitor-General 1885-6 ; Under-Secretary for India 1886-91 ; elected Hon. Fellow of St John's 1890 ; M.P. for the University 1892-1906.

HENRY ARTHUR MORGAN (1830-1912).
Jesus ; M.A. 1856, D.D. 1887, Fellow, Tutor and Master 1885-1912.
Morgan rowed in first boat many years c. 1851-60, and was Captain of the College Boat Club in Oct. 1851 and May 1853.   He gave the clock-turret for the boat-house in 1885, when the college eight had been head of the river for ten years.   Affectionately remembered as " Black Morgan " to distinguish him from " Red Morgan " the tutor.

JAMES CLERK MAXWELL (1831-1879).
Peterhouse (from Oct. to end of Nov. 1850, and then went to Trinity) ; M.A. 1857 ; F.R.S. ; elected Fellow of Trinity 1855.   Cavendish Professor of Experimental Physics 1871 ; Adams Prizeman 1857 ; Rumford Medallist (Roy. Soc.) 1860.   Founded a Scholarship, in Experimental Physics.

ARCHIBALD LEWIN SMITH (1836-1901).
Trinity ; B.A. 1858 ; knighted 1883 ; Master of the Rolls 1900.
Smith rowed 4 in the inter-University race of 1857, 2 in 1858, and 3 in 1859.   In 1859 the Boat Race was rowed in a gale of wind, and the Cambridge boat sank between Barnes' Bridge and the finish.   Smith alone of the Cambridge crew could not swim, and continued rowing until he was rescued with difficulty.

HERBERT SNOW (1835-1910).
St John's ; M.A. 1860, B.D. 1881, D.D. 1882 ; Camden Medallist and Browne Medallist 1855 ; bracketed Senior Classic 1857 ; Fellow of St John's 1858-60 ; Assist. Master Eton 1858-74 ; Principal of Cheltenham College 1874-88 ; Vicar of St Luke's, Kentish Town 1888-89.   Author of various classical works.
Snow (who subsequently assumed the name of Kynaston) rowed 7 in the inter-University race of 1856 and stroke in 1857.   He was one of the original members of the A.D.C.

Samuel Butler (1835-1902).

St John's; B.A. 1859; twelfth classic, 1858; philosophical writer; author of *Erewhon* (1872) and other works.

Butler before becoming a writer contemplated taking Orders and abandoned the intention. Emigrated to New Zealand, 1859, and became a sheep-breeder. Returned to England 1864-5; studied painting and exhibited at Royal Academy.

Frederick Ducane Godman (1834-1919).

Trinity; D.C.L., F.R.S., M.R.I., Trustee of the Brit. Museum, and

Osbert Salvin (1835-1898).

Trinity; M.A., 1860, F.R.S. Strickland Curator of Birds, 1874-1882.

These two distinguished travellers and naturalists may be mentioned together. They were friends and joint Editors of *Biologia Centrali-Americana*, a work vast in bulk and in learning.

Arthur Robert Ward (1829-1884).

St John's; M.A. 1858; Curate of All Saints', Cambridge, 1856-60; Vicar of St Clement's, Cambridge, 1860-84.

Ward was the younger son of a wealthy London banker (a director of the Bank of England) and merchant, who was a great cricketer and owner of Lord's Cricket Ground. He inherited his father's cricketing prowess, and also the ownership of " Lord's," which a few years before his death he sold to the M.C.C. Elected President and Treasurer of the Cambridge University Cricket Club on 1 May, 1873, he appealed successfully for subscriptions to build the present pavilion and also for the formation of a reserve fund for acquiring the freehold of Fenners. His eldest brother, William George Ward, Fellow of Balliol College, Oxford, was one of the well-known leaders of the Tractarian movement at Oxford. He wrote a book called *The Ideal of a Christian Church;* this gave rise to his sobriquet of "Ideal Ward." When Ward came up to Cambridge he was at once nicknamed, in consequence of his extraordinary size and weight, " The *Real* Ward," in contrast to his brother's name. He was a very considerable musician, playing organ, clarionet and piano. Ward was well known to a large circle of friends and contemporaries.

Rev. Thomas George Bonney, St John's; M.A. 1859, B.D. 1867, Sc.D. 1884; F.R.S.; Fellow of St John's; Hon. Canon of Manchester; Hulsean Lecturer, 1884; President of Geological Society, 1884-86; Rede Lecturer, 1892; Vice-President Royal Society, 1899; President of British Association, 1910-11; Ex-President Alpine Club, etc.

In addition to the various distinctions mentioned above, Dr Bonney is one of the few who remember Upware in the days of the " Republic." In response to a pardonable desire to have his

R. W. Shooter Captn Cath Hall. Ap 23
C. H. T. W. Dow   "   "
J. D. Ashworth. Coxn   ..   ..

C. H. T. W. Dow   Cath Hall
R. W. Shooter — -
J W Earnshaw (Capt) — .
A. T. Mulleliff (Stoke) — — — .
J. D. Ashworth (Coxn)

Consul Sir Clarke
Josephus Barr Ellison
       Archiepiscopus
President Hartley   May 31.

G. J. Bostock. Iron Hall. July 9.10.

Porter, & Sausages much to
be admired. N.B. G.J.B.
would advise naturalists to
"look before they leap" a title
knowledge too of Latin is required.

A PAGE FROM THE VISITORS' BOOK.

recollections of the Club where he was an occasional visitor, he has been good enough to place at my disposal the following notes :

Of this Club, I have only a general recollection. I used to skate to Upware in hard frost and go there for geology and entomology in the summer, but never stayed the night. There was, however, a Club there about that time (1852-1856), or a little earlier, though whether it had rules and mode of election I do not know. Some very able men in Cambridge were members, such as C. J. Newbery of St John's, 3rd Wrangler, 1853, who died of a rapid consumption in 1861 ; Joseph Wolstenholme of Christ's, 3rd Wrangler 1850 ; I think Du Port of Caius (1853) and Horne of St John's (1854) ; with other men about that standing. They went down occasionally to the Five Miles from Anywhere—No Hurry for a few days holiday, fishing in the Cam, or shooting on its banks, and talking in the evening with their rustic acquaintances. I do not know whether the Club was formally dissolved, or died " a natural death," after I returned to Cambridge in 1861. But I was not intimate with any of its members, and have only a general recollection of its history. A more complete change from Cambridge than it must have given, especially in the 'fifties, could not readily be conceived.

Came in a Trap.

SKETCH FROM THE VISITORS' BOOK.

The Upware Visitors' Book contains much more than a mere list of names. It is enlivened by an infinite variety of notes, stray scraps of information, narratives of adventure and personal observations relating, amongst other matters, to boating, shooting, fishing, natural history, excursions by land and water, convivialities and social gatherings, and, if wisdom is not conspicuous on every page, at least the whole volume is instinct with the exuberant vitality and irrepressible high spirits of youth.

Here are some of the more interesting of these records of happy days[1] :

BOATING.

The two visitors [J. W. Turnbull and J. K. Laughton] having arrived at Upware after a perilous voyage from Cambridge in their respective " funnies " ! ! ! hereby take solemn oath that if spared to return from the priest-ridden " Isle of Ely " they will burn to the Holy Virgin of Upware a " long six " or a " short dip." P.S. They hope on their return to be able to render a favourable account of the morality of the inhabitants of the aforesaid Isle.   (28 Jan. 1852.)

The two visitors have returned and accordingly must in consequence of their oaths burn a candle to the Virgin of Upware. In their opinion Ely is only second to Norwich for dirt and for a very peculiar low state of society. Malt liquors on the whole pretty fair. Egg-flip good if caution be given against curdling. Shell-fish supposed to be abundant—May Heaven preserve them (the visitors) from the Holy Trinity. (29 Jan. 1852.)

The men [T. L. Symes, T. C. Smyth, R. Fowler, and C. Sherlock] did a four oared boat at the imminent peril of their flesh and bones, in order to do a devil of a dinner of pork meat chops and beer liquor to the satisfaction of their souls, one man wore tail coat clothes which was borrowed in consequence of being wet with sweat.   (5 Mar. 1852.)

Left Searls in 1st Trinity 4 oar at 10¼ arrived at Upware ¼ before 12 ; found the household in thriving condition. [A. Calvert, G. B. Forster, J. J. Turner, A. Highton, and W. E. East.]   (29 Mar. 1852.)

The party . . . left Cambridge on Easter Monday [28 March, 1853] at 10.30 a.m. in Crosse's Barge (" Victoria ") on their way to Lynn, which place they reached at noon the following day, after a serious mishap at Downham Bridge. A few days of great jollity were spent at Lynn, and the party started homewards on Friday, Apr. 1st, at 10 a.m. This was a very boisterous day, and the " Victoria " was the only vessel that ventured to leave Lynn Harbour. Shortly after leaving Lynn, she lost her Union Jack and Dingy, and by a sudden lurch one man was cast overboard. After a rough 4 mile passage she was of necessity moured off at German's

---

[1] Printed absolutely without alteration.

till the next tide. Leaving this last place at 7 p.m. and sailing all night, she reached Upware at 11 a.m. on Saturday Apr. 2. The party were all much benefited by their Cruise.

The Lynn party wish to call particular attention to the heroic conduct of the famed Swidge [*i.e.* Charles Taylor of Swaffham], who on hearing of the excursion, *walked* with only a " Tizzy " in his pocket the whole way from Swaffham to Lynn, 40 miles, on Thursday, Mar. 31 and rendered very important service on the home passage. (28 Mar. 1853.)

Came in four-oar, dined, and spent a jolly evening, left at 8 in excellent preservation. [George Hogarth, W. Webb, C. A. R. Browning, and A. T. Millichap.] (30 Mar. 1853.)

An " out " jolly sail very squally, stopped all day, did a chop dinner, quoits and paddy's songs to follow, departed 5.30 for Camb. [A. D. Claydon, E. A. Claydon, and Wm. Eaden.] (1 April 1853.)

4.30 p.m. having returned from Ely in a pair oar. Left Cambridge at 7.30 this morning. Enjoyed a capital cold dinner at the Bell Hotel, where the fare is excellent, the beer good and the charges moderate. [J. Courè and Jack Fisher.] (4 Sept. 1854.)

Sculled in a " Funny " to Ely " Baked " " no End." Left Ely in the " Tiddledy Widdledy " thing as the natives termed it and sculled by moonlight to the " Five Miles "—Here turned in—" done up "—regular bricks here and no mistake. [H. E. F. Tracey.] (31 Mar. 1855)

2 Tub from Cross's to Upware where we enjoyed some of Mrs Appleby egg-flip—2 hours down—pulling—sail back. D. V. Adieu. [R. W. Shooter, C. H. T. W. Daw and J. D. Ashworth.] (23 April 1855.)

SHOOTING.

Fell in with a flock of rare Linnets (Linaria montium)[1] and shot about 50 ; lunched ; adjourned to the Fen and killed four Owls (strix Brachyitus) . . . [R. A. Julian, E. Outram, " Gaffer " [G. C.] Green, H. C. Stuart, and G. H. Wayte.] (8 Mar. 1852.)

Two members of the Cambridge University Naturalist Society arrived at Upware this day. Shot many Brambling Finches (Fringilla montium) and saw a male Hen-Harrier at Reach. [R. A. Julian and R. Ashley.] (25 Feb. 1853.)

[1] The Twite (*Linota flavirostris*, L.).

Fine day, came down in early dawn—when Aurora was just peeping o'er the borders of the renowned fen of Wicken. After a great deal of trouble we killed 9½ couple of Snip and Water-rails, and a remarkable pied variety of the stockdove. . . . [O'Hara Moore, R. Ashley, and H. K. Creed.] (2 Apr. 1853.)

Fen full of Snipe, and very wet, 4 guns—14 couple. [E. Outram, H. K. Creed, J. Williamson, and R. Ashley.] (15 Oct. 1853.)

We had an excellent day's sport, we killed 13 couple of Snipe, 6 Wild Duck, 3 Quails, 1 Partridge, 1 Hare, 3 Rabbits and several other little feathered monsters. [J. H. Hoblyn and F. S. Thorp.] (9 Nov. 1853.)

Came for a day's Snipe shooting, but went home with but 2 couple: found fen very dry, ditto Sportsmen, returned to Cambridge after a capital lunch. [J. Wright, F. Du Cane Godman, and C. F. Cornwall.] (16 Feb. 1856.)

FISHING.

Fishing very good. [C. Dix.] (3 Apr. 1855.)

Had an excellent day's sport fishing, . . . caught (including an eight pounder) 38lbs. weight of pike. [Ex-Consul Jennings, President Hartley, and H. F. Jackson.] (7 Apr. 1855.)

Sojourned for the space of ten days at the head-quarters of the Upware Republic. The excellent sport in the way of fishing (having captured 24lbs. of Jack in two days) and jovial ease of Upware Society combined with the well-known hospitality of Tom and the Missus caused these two latest made members of the Upware Republic to have much reluctance at leaving. [A. H. Hutton and D. M. Hunter.] (9-21 Apr. 1855.)

40lb. of Jack in 2 days. [Ex-Consul Jennings.] (23 Mar. 1856.)

SKATING.

The severe frost still continues, there has been skating the whole way from Grantchester to Littleport. . . . [E. G. Harvey.] (7 Jan. 1854.)

Skated from Waterbeach in 17'. Splendid ice! [J. Fisher, A. Ford, and S. Butler.] (10 Feb. 1855.)

Started from Cambridge at 2 o'clock, skating, and arrived here accordingly. [H. L. Todd, A. J. H. Bull, and J. Hayward.] (13 Feb. 1855.)

Skating from Ely.   [Consul-man Newbery.]   (19 Feb. 1855.)

Skated from Cambridge.   [Consul-man Newbery and N. Neville.]
                                                   (22 Feb. 1855.)
Turned in here on ye way up fr. Ely
left ye Railway Bridge at 1.45
reached Ely at 3.25
Upware at 4.30
N.B.   Hot ale not bad about this time after skating.
[J. C. Browne and C. G. Leslie.]   (22 Dec. 1855.)

CONVIVIALITIES.

Treasurer man Martin paid his Farewell visit to Upware, on this occasion deeply regretting that he was so soon destined to leave for ever a spot so charming and delightful.   At the same time he sincerely wishes political and commercial prosperity to the Upware Republic and earnestly entreats her future officers to uphold her dignity, power, and government as by law established, quite, altogether, completely, by the consent of the members.   (1 Mar. 1852.)

Consul Jennings paid his last visit to Upware on this day.   He quite agrees in sentiment with his friend the late Treasurer who a short time back recorded his own farewell to Upware, and he earnestly hopes that the Society may long flourish in the University, and find the same enjoyment in the pursuits, situation, harmony, and company of Upware and its environs which he has experienced for the last three years.   He cannot let this opportunity pass without stating his conviction that this enjoyment has been, in his own case, greatly increased by the many qualities of the excellent Vice-Consul and Mrs Appleby—that it will be so in the case of other he does not hesitate to predict.   (21 Mar. 1852.)

After a night's dancing and other such simple enjoyments as are furnished by a village feast—at Burwell. [Consul Jennings and Ex-Consul Wolstenholme.]   (17 May 1853.)

Arrived at 5 a.m. after an official and ex-official visit to Waterbeach feast. [Ex-Consul Wolstenholme and Consul Sin Clarke.]   (1 June 1853.)

Came down in a trap and met the full compliments of the season between here and Waterbeach for our pains. [President Newbery and Tapster Hartley.]   (1 Apr. 1854.)

The " hosses " . . . came down to Upware, purposely to revisit past scenes. They stopped several days, killing snipe, water-hens and such. They enjoyed themselves much—partly from the natural beauties of the place and partly from the pleasures of an affectionate " reunion " they being mostly diamonds and people as lived in the water. The Xtian " Hoss " finding a surley specimen of humanity in the shape of 20 stone of a fen farmer in a " Wossel " Field. The fat party turning up surley " The Diamond " beat an orderly retreat accordingly.

Flumina sylvasque inglorii amemus[1]

The wide wide fens are drear and cold
And drear and cold the weather
But the skies are light and the fens are bright
When warm hearts meet together.
H. K. C[reed].

[E. Outram, H. K. Creed, R. C. Healy, and A. G. Black, members of the C.U.N.S.]   (16 Oct. 1854.)

Not having been here since the foundation of the Republic, I am delighted to find that Upware still retains that pre-eminence amongst the fisheries of the Fens, which she enjoyed in the times of her ancient monarchs Floreat Upware. Long live the Queen. [Arthur C. Barrett, M.A.]
(9 Apr. 1855.)

The Ex-Consul before leaving Upware after a short but most agreeable visit wishes to express his satisfaction at finding the Republic in such a flourishing condition, he trusts that it may long continue so and never fail to give delight to those enlightened members of the University who honour it with their presence.

With reference to the remarks of the late " Count of Upware and Beach " entered a few pages back, he was only to observe that no memorial is necessary for one who has rendered himself immortal by the inscriptions outside the house and on the pewter. [Ex-Consul Jennings, M.A., and T. R. Powhele.]   (17 Apr. 1855.)

May 14th, 1856 (four days after the Independent comes out) Wednesday in Whitsun week.

Present Ex-Consul Jennings, Senior Acting Consul Clarke, President Hartley, Counsel Jackson, L.I., E. F. Holley, members who said this that and the other and when they opened their mouths had nothing to say.

---

[1] Cf. *Flumina amem silvasque inglorius*, Virg. G. ii., 486.

On arriving at the conclusion of this all important book, the above mentioned officers cannot refrain from looking back with great satisfaction to the many pleasant visits they have paid to Upware during the 4 years which are chronicled in this volume. They also look forward with confidence to the next visitors' book as the mirror of many future happy days at Upware.

Thus abruptly falls the curtain upon the Society's recorded history. Ten years later we find that singular and eccentric character, Richard Ramsay Fielder, M.A., of Jesus College, proclaiming himself " King of Upware," and challenging to combat those who ventured to dispute his assumed sovereignty over this riverside resort.

He was of a good family and of no mean ability, though with a gipsy nature and a decided antipathy to work. Here, at the old Lord Nelson Inn, familiarly known to us as the Five Miles from Anywhere—No Hurry, he lived and lounged for many years, a conspicuous figure in red waistcoat and corduroy breeches, drinking or fighting with the bargees as his strange humour led him. According to a contemporary :

He used to take about with him in his boat an enormous brownware jug, capable of holding six gallons or more, which he would at times have filled with punch, ladling it out profusely for his aquatic friends. This vast pitcher or " gotch " which was called " His Majesty's pint " (in allusion to his self-assumed title), had been made to his own order, and decorated before kilning with incised ornaments by his own hand. Amongst these figured prominently his initials " R.R.F.," and his crest, actual or assumed, a pheon, or arrow-head.

At Earith, and in the Jenyns' Arms at Denver may be seen memorials of this pot-house monarch, and various sets of doggerel verses, printed for the most part on single leaves, still survive. I have in my possession two pamphlets, one entitled *Lines written for the Tercentenary Anniversary Festival* (of Shakespeare's birth) . . . by His Majesty of Upware. . . . Ely 1871, also a fly-leaf entitled *Ode to the Prince of Wales, and Princess Alexandra of Denmark*, by His Majesty of Upware, Ely 1863. The last has a footnote in Fielder's handwriting stating that it was reprinted in 1871.

The following extract from his lines on Shakespeare will give some idea of Fielder's powers of versification :

> As mine unworked which holds the precious ore,
> Our language was, or feebly wrought before ;
> His daring first the rugged depths explored,
> Minted the wealth, and left a priceless hoard ;
> And the impress he stamped for current speech,
> Still keeps the value he assigned to each.
>
> .   .   .   .
>
> O ! were I wrecked upon some coast alone,
> Within the tropic, or the frozen zone,
> With THINE, and with that other BOOK, endued,
> Such limits could not be—a Solitude.

With the advent of the railway most of the river-traffic ceased, and with it the hefty bargees. Fielder's associates gone, report tells that he " forswore sack and lived cleanly," retiring to Folkestone, where, in due time and in the odour of sanctity, he died.

Gone are the old roystering days at Upware and with them the picturesque reed-thatched roof of its once-famed Inn, now replaced by corrugated iron.

During the Great War, the Inn was utilised for the accommodation of German prisoners. Windows were broken, and with the panes disappeared names scratched upon the glass, which would have been lost for ever but for the happy recovery of this Visitors' Book of the Upware Republic.

Guide Map of the Borough of Cambridge

Published by W. HEFFER AND SONS, LTD., CAMBRIDGE.

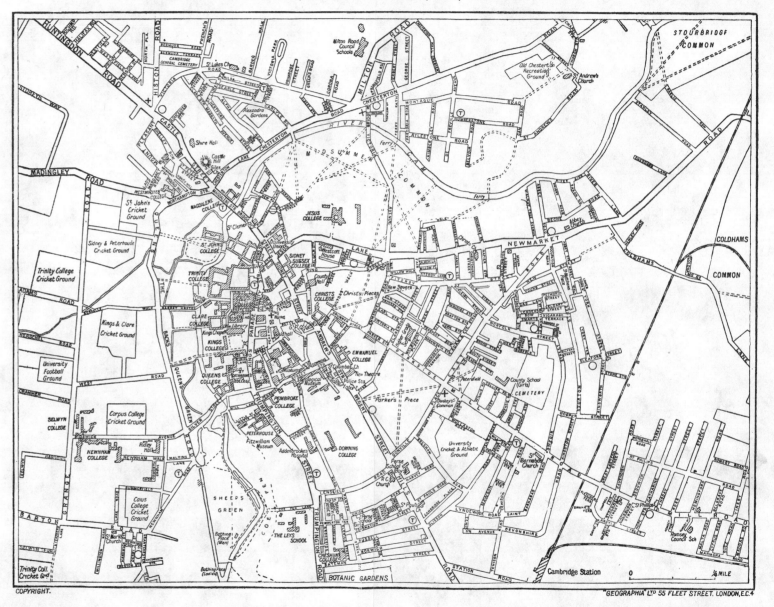

COPYRIGHT.

"GEOGRAPHIA" LTD 55 FLEET STREET. LONDON, E.C.4

Index

INDEX